THE WRITER'S GUIDE TO THE BUSINESS OF COMICS

THE WRITER'S GUIDE TO THE BUSINESS OF COMICS

LURENE HAINES

Watson-Guptill Publications
New York

Senior Editor: Candace Raney
Editor: Margaret Sobel
Designer: Jay Anning
Production Manager: Ellen Greene

Library of Congress Cataloging-in-Publication Data
Haines, Lurene
    The writer's guide to the business of comics: everything a comic book writer
needs to make it in the business—: plus interviews with 40 comic book
professionals/Lurene Haines.
        p.   cm.
    Includes bibliographical references and index.
    ISBN 0-8230-5877-8
    1. Comic books, strips, etc.-Authorship-Marketing. 2. Comic books, strips, etc.-
Marketing. I. Title.
    PN6714.H348   1998
    808'.066741-dc21   98-25961
                                                     CIP

Printed in the USA

First Printing, 1998

1 2 3 4 5 6 7 8 9/04 03 02 01 00 99 98

For writers who dream and dreamers who write.

Acknowledgements

I would like to express my appreciation for the patience and invaluable assistance of the folks who helped me to bring this book to completion.

First, I would like to thank Candace Raney of Watson-Guptill Publications. Candace had the vision to recognize the usefulness and potential of my comics business books. I appreciate her confidence in the work.

I would also like to thank Margaret Sobel, my editor on the book. Margaret is unfailingly considerate and terrific at dealing with authors. I value her soothing, level-headed calm.

Thanks also to Gary Reed of Caliber Comics whose support made my enthusiastic ideas possible in the first place.

I would also like to thank Jamie Riehle of Kitchen Sink Press, Barry Branvold (a willing and abundantly helpful research resource who always makes me laugh), and Steve Sibra—the former owner of Rocket Comics in Seattle, Washington, and freelance entrepreneur.

Finally, I would like to thank the many professionals who agreed to take part in the book and provided me with supplemental information. The pros I interviewed for this book were cooperative, extraordinarily helpful, and very patient. For all of this I thank everyone most sincerely.

CONTENTS

APPENDIXES

AN OVERVIEW OF THE INDUSTRY

"My son has created a whole universe of characters—I think he's up to 280 now—can you publish his stories?"

"I've tried every single publisher, but they just won't look at my completed mini-series script!"

"I know I've got a comic script that will blast other writers out of the water!"

"Can you just read this quickly, and tell me who will publish it?"

"All I want to do is write comics. Where do I start?"

Many comic professionals have heard a barrage of these types of comments and questions. What it all comes down to is that many aspiring writers do not have a clue about how to write for comics, or the business machinations of this industry.

WHAT IS THE BUSINESS OF COMICS?

The comic book industry has been an active part of our culture for more than 50 years. Although in the past the comic book was primarily a form of entertainment for kids, it has since evolved into a more diverse form of entertainment, appealing to both young and old alike, and has generated a highly successful collector's market. Besides all that, the comic book represents an alternative form of expression and creativity for many people.

Many potential writers are just itching to try their hand at generating their own unique interpretation of a comic book story. So just how do they break into the business?

Take a serious look at your own likes and dislikes. Decide if writing for comics is going to hold your interest down the road. Any kind of freelancing is a lot of work—it's not a 40-hour-a-week job. This is going to be your whole life, especially the first few years when you are establishing yourself. Be sure that you'll be happy with what you're doing. Don't approach it cynically, thinking, "I'm going to do whatever it takes because I want to make a lot of money." Chances are you're not going to make a lot of money in this business. There are very few "superstars." Most of us, if we stick with it, make a decent living. But given the amount of work we put into it, we could make a much better living doing something else. You've got to love this business to be in it.

MARK SCHULTZ
Artist/Author

GETTING INTO THE BUSINESS

This book is not designed to instruct you on how to develop your writing talents. Instead, I offer business advice and suggestions for honing those skills. I assume that you feel you have reached a skill level adequate to pursue comic book writing. I propose ways for you to find out where your abilities stand in relation to industry requirements, and hopefully provide some useful advice on how to deal with critiques and professional feedback.

Ultimately, however, this book deals with the *business* of getting writing jobs by shedding light on a variety of areas crucial for doing business as a writer in the comic industry. Many of the suggestions apply to related career fields, and you may want to consider reading more about those industries. Some of the information is common sense. If you find the material is familiar, move on. There is plenty of information useful to aspiring comic writers of all levels of expertise.

In the time I've been a comic professional, I've worked very hard and tried to stay on top of all the latest business and professional information. I attend dozens of conventions and make numerous appearances each year, and at every one, without fail, some eager—though often timid—aspiring writer will approach me with what might appear to be the silliest question with the most obvious answer.

But if I've learned nothing else, I've learned to respect the courage it took to ask a question that might seem dumb to everyone else. I answer them as honestly and fully as I can, and always with good humor.

And that's what I hope to do here in this book. I have broken down the various aspects of writing for comics, and the different routes and methods you can utilize to make sure you have the greatest chance of securing your dream career.

Read a lot more than just comic books. The industry is awash with writers whose entire literary experience is comic books and action movies. Writers should be reading newspapers, magazines—anything and everything. Because if they only read comic books, we're just going to get rehashes of old comic books instead of new stories.

TONY ISABELLA
Writer/Columnist

BEING A PROFESSIONAL

There are a number of tools for maximizing your chances of getting work in the comic industry. You should utilize as many of these as you can.

Enthusiasm is indispensable. If you truly love what you do, then you'll write stories that you're happy with, which will inspire you even further. That kind of enthusiasm can be contagious, as well. Other professionals like to deal with someone who clearly enjoys their work. Nothing can put you off a business deal faster than someone who doesn't share your enthusiasm or excitement for a project. But remember to keep it under control. Hyper-excitement is just as much a put-off as total lethargy!

D.G. Chichester, Writer/Editor/multimedia kinda-guy
Credits Include: *Marshal Law* and *Hellraiser* (editing) from
Marvel/Epic; *Big Numbers* (production manager) from Mad Love
Press; *Punisher/Captain America: Blood and Glory* (with Margaret
Clark), *Feivel Goes West* comic adaptation, *Daredevil, Terror, Inc.,*
Elektra: Root of Evil and *Daredevil: Original Sin* (writer) all for
Marvel Comics; *Classics Illustrated: Moby Dick* (with Bill Sienkiewicz)
for First Comics; the *Motorhead* series from Dark Horse Comics;
Primal and *Dark Lotus* screenplays (with Erik Saltzgaber).

Question: Do you believe that educational and/or experiential
background in the writing field is valuable when trying to acquire
work in the comic industry?

Yes, I believe that kind of background is going to be valuable if it is applied
toward comics. You can have a background in screenwriting or education, for
example, and try to bring it into comics. But if you do not apply it to the
specifics of the medium, you're going to be lost. I think a writing background
allows you to bring something new to the comics genre. Having something new
to add from your personal experience or knowledge, in terms of approach or
content, means that you are going to be unique to the editor or artist that you
are working with. You won't be treading over the same old tired ground.

However, it can be a bit of a double-edged sword. If you come in with this
alternative experience or knowledge, people might assume you don't know
about the specifics of comics. They may think that if you don't have a
background in comics, you can't possibly understand how things are done. That's
why I think you've got to be able to apply that education or experience to the
specifics of comics. I don't think you can come into the industry without being
familiar with the characters or the marketplace that you're trying to break into,
whether it's superheroes, horror, funny animal-type books, or traditional dramas.
You've got to know what's out there. If you can do that, and also bring
something new to it, you will make yourself that much more valuable. A richer
background will only provide richer and more diverse comics.

With regards to specific background or education I think—and this comes out
of my own background—that an understanding and appreciation of film (the
techniques or tools of film and the structures of screenwriting)—can be

particularly valuable for comics. But, again, it must to be applied to the specifics of the genre.

If you just try to take the film approach to screenwriting and try to apply it directly to comics, you're going to end up with a very stilted book and a comic that does not take advantage of the unique qualities of the medium. By the same token, at least for the time being, the closest and most readily translatable language for comics comes from film. Picking up bit of film language and using it in comics can be extremely useful. It really helps you from a writing standpoint to appreciate what happens to the written word, in terms of translating it into visuals and how the pacing and the rhythm affect your story. It can make the whole difference between 22 pages that fill an issue and 22 pages that have that special rhythm and pacing that create drama and effect, so that when you get to the end of a three-page sequence, the reader is literally on the edge of their seat because the writer was able to pull all the elements altogether.

Granted, the art can be paramount—it may break a good story if it's no good—but if you don't provide the material in the first place, then the artist has nothing to work with and you've failed in your job. So if you want to consider an educational background, film training can be useful.

As for experience, anything you've done—as a fireman, cop, short-order cook, comic store retailer—any experience you have, can help. Also use research. I'm a big believer in research, whether it's reading 18 books or going and hanging out at a local mall for three days to pick up specific bits of dialogue. The whole trick I think, for many types of comics, is to take a certain aspect of reality and put a twist on it. Not enough comics writers do that. But I think that having that taste of reality provides a strong, believable hook that will lead the reader into the rest of the strange world the writer has created. As opposed to just saying, "This is my Matter Transmorgifier!" Well, what the hell is that? If you're able to base the premise, for example, on a real Department of Defense experiment, from which you can quote a couple of actual statistics because you've done the research (or were involved in the experiment), you can provide a story that has that extra ring of truth to it. And if you have a nominal command of the language, you can convey that to the reader, artist, and editor, and that is ultimately going to create a better story and better opportunities for yourself.

You should also bring your own personal work experience to bear in the comics industry. Being a comics writer isn't the first job I've ever held, and I've found that many business techniques and methods I've used in other jobs have had great application here. Any type of writing experience adds to your expertise. When getting started, it pays to write a variety of comics-related material as a sort of "training ground." But remember, the writing experience you bring from other fields is also beneficial.

Don't be afraid to ask questions. People will respect you for wanting to do a good job. But remember, if you can look up the answer, do it! There's nothing that will shake confidence in you faster than the appearance of being perpetually confused.

Probably the most important method for improving your chances of getting work, and becoming a true professional is your ability to listen. I mean really listen. Every time a business professional gives me advice, I pay attention. Often they haven't imparted any startlingly new insight, but they almost always give me a whole new perspective on that information, which makes a big difference when I approach a business problem the next time around.

Hopefully this book will provide you with a whole new perspective as well as a lot of new and useful information.

If you want to "make it" in comics, then leave your artistic integrity at the door and sign a pact with the devil before entering the "Fun House."

MARK RICKETTS
Writer/Illustrator

A LOOK AT THE INDUSTRY

From a professional standpoint, we're very fortunate to have such a wide and diverse comics market in which to work. As a freelancer, this provides a broad source of publishing houses to choose from, adding variety and generating a satisfying degree of competitiveness.

As of October 1998, there were more than 140 different companies actively soliciting published material. Of those publishers, over 20 are well-known, and a substantial number are exclusively self-publishing. Of the better known companies, the top four publishers are (in alphabetical order) DC Comics, Dark Horse Comics, Image Comics, and Marvel Comics.

Where to Begin

Presumably, you have already taken a stab at producing some sort of sample or work. Either you have had classes and are producing material for scholastic requirements and homework, or you've been practicing on your own. With your writing samples in hand, you're ready to start. But where to begin—who should you approach with your beloved ideas?

Many newcomers look at the market, and see only the big, high-profile companies. But it's important to know a few things before you approach a potential publisher. You need to decide if that publisher would be willing to publish your work and if they can offer you more than "just getting published." Established pros are always hearing, "I've always dreamed of writing my favorite comic book character!"

These naive newcomers are certain that just presenting an editor or publisher with their "golden" idea will guarantee that they're "discovered."

Nope. It's not gonna happen.

In reality, sending unsolicited material alone is generally insufficient to garner a writing job in the comic industry. Particularly if the aspiring newcomer fails to follow acceptable form and procedure or if their work is unpolished. And especially, if in combination with those things, the newcomer is an unproven commodity.

An unproven commodity simply means that publishers generally want a recognizable "Name"—an established or fan-favorite professional—to help sell their books. Now that's not always the case. But publishing, as I've already pointed out, is a highly competitive business. With the flood of new and small publishers, and the glut of generated collectibles, the comics market has suffered some economic blows. A significant number of retailers have succumbed to the collector frenzy of 1992–93, when speculation reached an all-time high, and retailers bowed to customer wishes and ordered massive quantities of books that, ultimately, did not sell well enough. Many were driven out of business by their poor judgment in investing in the collector products produced by greedy comics publishers and have since gone out of business. As a result, publishers are fiercely competing with each other for the ever-slimmer market share. Therefore, anything that will help draw attention to a new book means more sales and a bigger share. That often means using a Name.

ProFile

Neil Gaiman, Writer
Credits Include: *Black Orchid, Death: The High Cost of Living, Sandman* series and collections, *Violent Cases, Mr. Punch, The Last Temptation* from DC Vertigo; *Signal to Noise* (illustrated by Dave McKean) from Gollancz and Dark Horse Comics; *Miracleman: The Golden Age* from Eclipse and HarperCollins; *Angels and Visitations* (prose) from DreamHaven.

Question: Do you believe that on-line computer services are of value to aspiring comics writers?

When you use them for research, for sending long faxes and e-mails to a bunch of different people, or for arranging travel, yes, undoubtedly. But the rest of the time, on-line services are an expensive way to kill time, and a way of persuading yourself you're working when you're not. They're more fun, and more educational, than playing Tetris or Solitaire.

On the other hand, because the comic industry has experienced some difficult financial times, some publishers are more willing to experiment with a newcomer who commands a lesser salary. Ultimately, however, fewer pros are being hired in general, because of reduced publisher earnings. This will make your job of securing work even more difficult.

Anyway, back to the Name. Just how does a professional become a Name?

Well, it varies from case to case, and depends on when the professional's career started. The way things were done 20, 30, or 40 years ago contrasts dramatically

ProFile

Steve Englehart, Writer
Credits Include: One of the seven founding Ultraverse writers for Malibu Comics; *Strangers* and *Nightman* from Malibu Comics; *Captain America, Dr. Strange, Master of Kung Fu, Silver Surfer, Vision* and the *Scarlet Witch, Fantastic Four* from Marvel Comics; *Millennium, Batman, Green Lantern Corps, Justice League of America* from DC Comics; *Coyote, Scorpio Rose* from Eclipse and Epic.

Question: Is there anything specific you think newcomers should keep in mind as they approach a career in comics?

The thing I think that people need to keep in mind as they're making a career in comics, is what gets said a lot in international diplomacy: "Trust but verify." I would extrapolate that to "trust but verify, and then trust some more." Everybody should have some feeling that what they're doing is worth doing. Why it shouldn't be somebody else doing this job. Why it should be you. Inevitably, along the line in your career, you're going to run into both well-meaning and ill-meaning people, who are going to say things like, "You don't know what you're talking about! You're living in an illusion. You're not as good as you think you are, etc., etc." The human thing and the easy thing to do, particularly if you've done the first part—which is to figure out why you're cool—is to say, "That guy's a jerk. I'm not going to pay any attention to him." But I don't think that is a valuable way to go. The guy may be a jerk, but the point is you've got to look at the problem a little more deeply than that. You've got to say, "Alright, here is somebody's criticism of my work that I'm trying to build my career on. Is there any validity to it?" You've got to be honest with yourself. If the guy's right, then you've got to say, "He's right. This is something that I can't do, or can't do now." From there you have to decide if you can learn how to do it, how to make it better. Just throwing away all negative with what is now accepted form.

Newer professionals got their breaks in a variety of ways. Some started out by working hard as an assistant to an established pro who then acted as their mentor—a variation of schooling and on-the-job training. Others began in editorial departments and worked their way up. This is often an excellent starting place for writers. However, not everybody lives in the city of a publisher or working pro. The very nature of our business allows for professionals to live wherever they choose and send in their work.

comments out-of-hand is not going to help you improve on a professional or a personal level.

Roy Thomas once said that Stan Lee could be devastated by a postcard. He'd get one negative letter, and he'd say, "Oh my God, we're screwed!" And this was at Marvel Comics' height of popularity! I think that as a self-employed professional, you need to walk a line between believing in yourself and wanting to know if you're not doing it right. The point is to keep walking the line and not fall off on either side. You don't want to think, "They're all right, and I'm awful." But you also don't want to be thinking, "They're all wrong, and I'm perfect."

Ultrascarce: *Comic cover parody*

If you take the stance that you're right and everyone else is wrong, you're not likely to build the kind of networking skills that you need to keep going.

I would say, trust in yourself and verify what other people say. After that, trust in yourself again. When you have taken an honest look at what people have to say, and you've decided that they're right and you'll do better, or they're wrong and you're comfortable with that decision, then go back to believing in yourself.

Anyone approaching this field as a career option should be aware that knowing nothing can be an asset. When I began in comics, I knew absolutely nothing. If ignorance is bliss, I was downright rapturous when I embarked on my comics career. In hindsight, I wonder if having access to insights of industry professionals would have enhanced my career or abruptly halted it. I certainly know now that it was even more profound ignorance that lured me, without preparation, into the jungles of publishing. Ignorance allowed me to do things and accomplish things that conventional wisdom would have discouraged at the start.

DENIS KITCHEN
Publisher, Kitchen Sink Press, Inc.

THE SMALL PRESS AND SELF-PUBLISHING

Given the previously mentioned limitations, how does one get started? That's where the "small press" and self-publishing come in.

Many professionals will gladly tell you that almost NOBODY starts at the top. Like anything else in life, there are exceptions to every rule, but very few of these in our own cherished industry. You'll find that you're going to have to start humbly and work your way up. For many folks, humbly means the mailroom at the publisher of your choice. Well, that's fine if you're interested in handling mail and if you already happen to live in that publisher's city. However, what I mean by humbly is a willingness to start small and work your way up. Starting small as a writer in the comic industry means that sometimes the opportunity to be published by a lesser-known company can provide you with both exposure and an opportunity to improve your writing skills while your work is published—in other words, on-the-job training!

Of the 140-plus publishers in our industry, about 85 percent of those are small independents or self-publishing companies. A few got started as vanity presses ("I have a comic I want to publish and nobody else wants it, so I'll do it myself!"); some are offshoots of larger companies ("We are pleased to introduce our Alternative Comics line."); some are foreign press ("Those Americans have no taste in comics. Let's show them what real comic art looks like—and make some bucks!"); some handle only reprint material ("Well, we've got all these great books around from about 20 years ago. Let's sell them to this new audience."); and some just pop up ("I inherited/swindled/borrowed all this money, so I think I'll publish comics.") Whatever the reason for their existence, what they represent is a fertile publishing market, and a great selection of publishers to choose from.

Many self-publishing companies are founded only so a particular aspiring professional can get his or her work published. Sometimes when people write comics that are so alternative and they have trouble finding a publisher willing to chance the financial investment, they choose to publish it themselves. Often they can be wildly successful.

Some self-publishers produce their own book because publishers deem it insufficiently polished to generate consumer interest. Sometimes they can be successful, although more often they manage to produce only one or two issues before they go out of business.

Some self-publishers start to publish so they can completely control the final product. They are interested in controlling their creator rights. The issue of creator rights is a divisive one in the comics industry, but many self-publishers have found a marked degree of success and happiness by pursuing this avenue.

In all three of these self-publishing cases, the companies generally only publish their own product and do not consider the work of others. Many times they are operating on a shoestring budget. Generally, self-publishers will not accept unsolicited submissions and are not actively seeking work to publish. However, there are other small companies who had started out as a self-publishing venture but found, due to financial success, that they were able to expand their publishing list to include material from other creators. It is always worthwhile to fully investigate the status of a company before pursuing work with them, to better determine your chances and the appropriateness of approaching that publisher.

For an unproven newcomer still honing his skills, the "small press" and some self-publishing companies mean good news. These publishers are generally working from a much smaller budget than those "big guys," and in general can't afford to hire a Name or many Names. From an economic viewpoint, that's not too great for an aspiring (and probably starving) writer. But with a bit of economic sacrifice these smaller publishers can furnish a proving ground, exposure to the industry and, best of all, published samples. These things will hopefully lead to the better paying jobs!

Know where you are at financially when you start out. The ideal situation is to keep another job from which you know you'll earn an income. Or, as in my case, have a spouse that works a regular job, and who can help support you while you're getting started. Learn to budget yourself and keep your overhead as low as possible. You're going to have to sacrifice and be frugal, so have a reservoir or some type of financial cushion that you can fall back on.

MARK SCHULTZ
Artist/Author

On the other hand, many professionals have nothing but glowing words about their economic arrangements with the independents. Some of these independent publishers offer attractive alternative financial agreements including a share of profits and substantial royalties instead of upfront page rates. Best of all, some independent publishers offer creator rights—something the "big guys" rarely offer (and most assuredly not to an unproven newcomer!). Factors that should dictate which publisher(s) you approach include the type of financial arrangement you can live with; whether exposure through publishing with that company will benefit you; how badly you want to keep the rights to characters you create; and just how desperately you want to be published.

Some of the better known independent companies include Antarctic Press, Caliber Comics, Chaos! Comics, Dark Horse Comics, Fantagraphics, Kitchen Sink Press, Sirius Entertainment, and Slave Labor Graphics. There is as much variation in their handling of writers, both in terms of rights and financial arrangements, as there is in the type of material they publish. It is up to you, as an aspiring comics writer, to inquire into what each company has available, should you choose to approach them for work.

The type of material, or genre, published by each company also varies. The two most recognized companies, Marvel and DC Comics, tend toward a lineup of popular superhero material. That's not to say these companies avoid alternative materials; they just tend to publish those works under a different banner-head (i.e., Vertigo and Piranha Press for DC Comics). These lines tend to follow the company policy in terms of financial arrangements, but sometimes offer more attractive, creator-rights agreements.

The other companies, or independents, publish products that range from conventional superhero to extremely experimental/cutting edge material. Frequently, it is this variation from the superhero genre that most appeals to a newcomer.

Organize and focus on where you want to work. If you want to submit something to a given editor, make sure you know which books that editor is working on. Submit something that is appropriate for one of those books. Every editor I know seems to have a screaming need for fill-in issues. Well, know how to do a fill-in issue, and submit something that is professional in appearance and appropriate for that editor's books. Don't give a Batman editor a Spider-Man plot and hope they'll see what a great writer you are!

JOHN OSTRANDER
Freelance Writer

HOW DO I GET STARTED?

With all of this information about money, exposure, and genre in mind, you should carefully examine the material published by each company. It's best to start out by doing some research of your own.

1. Spend some time at your local comic stores and newsstands. Don't stick to just one shop, but look around. Comic store owners and managers are fans, just like you, and they may have a tendency to order material they prefer, or only titles that are guaranteed hot sellers. If you check across a couple of shops you're bound to see a wider selection of books, and therefore you'll get a much better idea of what's out there, and with whom you'd like to do business.

2. Don't just look, ask questions. Most shop owners are glad to answer questions, and many are very knowledgeable about the business. Sometimes an articulate discussion with a store owner/manager can provide you with valuable insight into the stories and writing that excites them and their customers. Take note of their likes and dislikes, and use that information to analyze and improve your work. You will also glean information about which books, and hence publishers, are selling well. This type of information can be invaluable when pursuing work.

3. Ask if you can look at the distributor catalogs. Distributing companies handle the products produced by the publishers. They are the direct contact between the

Louise Simonson, Writer

Credits Include: *X-Factor, Power Pack, Meltdown, Web of Spider-Man, New Mutants, Red Sonja* from Marvel; *Batman, Teen Titans, Superman: Man of Steel, Steel* from DC Comics; *Star Wars* mini-series for Dark Horse. Her children's books include *Superman: Doomsday and Beyond* from Warner Books; *I Hate Superman* from Little Brown; *Superman* and *Wonder Woman* from Little Golden Books.

Question: Is there anything that you specifically recommend new writers avoid doing?

I would recommend that they not just read comic books. I would suggest that they not simply focus on the action of their stories, but focus on the characters and what's inside the hearts and minds of those characters.

Companies tell you to send a one-page synopsis of a plot, and that if they like it they will call you to do a story. I don't believe that works. I think if you do that, it might be fun for an exercise, but I wouldn't hold my breath. I don't know anyone who's ever gotten a job that way. I think you need to attend conventions and make personal contacts. Most of the people I know who are doing comics, who are writers now, were either working for the company in some other capacity—such as in the editorial department—or they worked outside of comics and began writing comics almost as an aside. Or they're artists.

Finally, I think people also have a tendency to target one company, and fail to submit anything to the competing companies. That's not a good idea. Don't restrict yourself.

Art from Superman: The Man of Steel Annual #4

publishers and the stores. They are responsible for providing order forms, processing the orders, and shipping the product. The catalogs, also called order books or solicitations, list all the material that is to be printed by every publisher for the next sales period. There is often a description of the books, and sometimes a detailed outline of the story that a particular issue will feature. Some are accompanied by samples of the issue's artwork, and a list of the creative team on the project. Take note of the companies that are utilizing freelance writers versus editorial staff writers and illustrators who write their own material. The distributor catalogs can provide some very useful research information, particularly if your local store fails to order from the more obscure companies.

4. Check out comic industry trade publications. Our industry plays host to a variety of informative comics news sources. Some of these include the weekly papers *The Comics Buyers Guide* and *Comic Shop News,* and monthlies *Wizard: The Guide to Comics, The Comics Journal,* and *Comics Scene.* Each of these publications offers a unique perspective on a variety of areas in the industry, including a good look at what's new from the various publishers. To be a knowledgeable professional (and to give yourself an advantage in doing business in the comics industry) it is in your best interest to read at least a couple of these trade publications regularly.

Treat getting a job writing comics as if it were a job in itself—it's not easy to get a job in any field and comic books are no exception. It requires talent, perseverance, contacts, follow-through, and more.

TOM MASON
Co-founder, MainBrain Productions

5. If you have access to the Internet, make use of the comics forums and news. In this increasingly technological age, you owe it to yourself as a professional to stay apprised in every way possible. Many of the popular computer on-line services such as America Online and Compuserve, offer comic-related information and forums. Additionally, many new informational web sites are added to the net every day. Make sure you check out the material that appears on-line on a daily basis. Many comics professionals utilize these services and make themselves available for discussions and Q & A. Their input and answers to your questions are a priceless resource.

6. Create a record of information on prospective publishers. This can take the form of a notebook, a loose-leaf binder, a card index, or a computer file. Just make note of a few pieces of pertinent information about the specific publishers that interest you. This information should include a variety of elements:

• Head your record entries with the company name, address and phone numbers.

• Make note of the names of any editors you wish to approach.

• Record information about the genre they tend to publish.

Mark Ricketts, Writer/illustrator/friend to cab drivers
Credits Include: *Warpwalking, International Cowgirl Magazine, Twilight People, Negative Burn, The Book of Twilight, Ghost Sonata, Deadworld, Thumbscrew,* and *High Caliber* for Caliber Press; *Urban Legends, Hellboy* pin-up for Dark Horse Comics.

Question: Do you believe that educational and experiential background is valuable when trying to acquire work in the comic industry?

Keep in mind, the comics industry's roster of writers comprises a diverse collection of former fanboys and girls ranging from the extremely educated, the extremely gifted, the extremely intuitive, right down to the just plain insipid, so there's likely to be a place for you!

Whatever the response, negative or ambivalent, keep sending out your new work. Bombard those publishers with your beautifully double-spaced, spell-checked visions, but be sure to make it concise. Nobody is expecting or wants a proposal of Proustian dimensions. Include one page for summary, and one page for character profiles. If they want to see a script or a fully fleshed out summary, they'll ask for it. I would recommend that you send your ideas for books to the independent publishers, but they usually want fully realized packages—words and pictures! If you can find an illustrator to interpret your writings you might have a better chance at being published. Also, it's not going to hurt to have a sequential artboy around telling you to "get visual." For those not lucky enough to find an art pal, watch *Citizen Kane* a couple of hundred times. If you find an illustrator, create a complete comic, and get published by an independent publisher, you may not get the financial reward you deserve (there are some exceptions). But the "Indies" are a great place to sharpen your teeth, hone your skills, and taste the sweet and sour of this business while you find your voice.

*From Rickett's
Book of Twilight*

- Note the style of their product (black and white vs. color, monthly book vs. mini-series, comics vs. graphic novels).

- List the recognizability of talent (i.e., do they tend to use Names, etc.)

- Who owns the rights to the characters? (Listed in the indicia.)

- What is the average cost of the books?

- Include any other information you discover and think would be helpful in deciding whether they would be interested in your work.

You can also expand this record to include information about publishers in related industries that interest you (i.e., the trade book market, TV and movie scripting, etc.). Use some of the various writer's market guides available to expand your information database.

What Now?

Now that you have a wealth of valuable information about your potential employers, you've gotten a truly professional start on your comics writing career. You've done some research. You know who is publishing material similar to what you have to offer. You also are aware of the caliber of work they're publishing, and the types of professionals they hire. If you're interested in working on superhero books, you now have a list of names to contact. If you want to pursue a character you've created, but don't want to give up your rights, you know which publisher honors creator rights.

Follow your bliss, don't give up, and don't take anything personally.

BILL MESSNER-LOEBS
Writer/Artist

Your next, and most important step is to send out requests for submissions guidelines.

Submissions Guidelines

Submissions guidelines are a written guide, produced by each individual publisher, which details the manner and format in which they will consider unsolicited material. Many publishers will not even contemplate new material unless the proposals follow the company guidelines for new submissions. Some companies don't have a structured set of guidelines, so just follow the most professional submissions procedure and direct your work to the Editor of New Submissions. In this way, you follow the most efficient company format, and your sample won't sit on a desk at the bottom of somebody's "To Do" stack or slush pile.

Here are the steps you should take to obtain a copy of a publisher's submissions guidelines:

1. Send a request letter. Your letter should be written in a businesslike manner. Ask for a copy of their submission guidelines. Keep the letter brief or it will not be read. State

THE SIX MOST COMMON WAYS OF BREAKING INTO COMICS

1. Be an employee with a comic publishing company. You're there. You're around. So when an editor who needs an eight-page fill-in comes looking, you're right there to make his or her search easier.

2. Be an artist. Artist's have leverage and can often get writing jobs if they show basic writing ability.

3. Know an artist. If you have a relationship with an established comics freelancer who is willing, then team up. If you have a friend who's trying to break in as an artist, team up. You're chances are greatly improved if you are coming in with the artist.

4. Be an editor or an assistant editor. These are the folks who ultimately decide who writes the stories. It's a lot easier to get the job if you're also the boss.

5. Make blind submissions. Although not always effective, this is a possible avenue. But artists are more frequently pulled from the submissions pile. Writers rarely are, since most editors have a stable of creators they work with, and tend to go back to them.

6. Do work for small companies and independents, including writing articles for industry publications. This gives you comic-book work to show editors. Some writers even got their start by submitting regular letters of comment to the "Letters to the Editor" page of their favorite comic book.

your request simply, and save the color and personal information for the cover letter accompanying your actual submission.

2. Include a self-addressed, stamped envelope (SASE) for the reply. Although it's not always required, the SASE is a business courtesy. Remember, publishers get hundreds of inquiries, so set yourself apart as a true professional—invest in a first-class postage stamp and #10 legal-sized envelope.

3. Send another letter if you haven't received a response within six weeks. Many publishers are heavily backlogged with work. If you have not received your requested copy of the guidelines within six weeks, send another letter, explaining that it is your second request and that you have yet to receive a response. Be polite, not demanding, and be sure to include another SASE. Just remember that it might not be the publisher's fault—maybe the post office is to blame! Be patient. Be professional.

4. Once the guidelines arrive, add the writer's information to your record on the company. This way you have a log of data from which to draw when making your

actual submissions—and a way to keep track of the companies you contacted, how you contacted them, and what the response was.

You may also acquire a copy of a company's submissions guidelines by accessing their web site on the Internet. Most major publishers, and many of the small companies, have their submissions guidelines posted for easy downloading. If you have access to the Internet, this is a quick and inexpensive way to immediately obtain this information. Web site addresses (URLs) for many companies are listed in Appendix C at the back of this book.

ProFile

John Moore, Writer
Credits Include: *American Flagg! Vol #2* from First Comics; *Superboy, Ironwolf: Fires of the Revolution* (with Howard Chaykin), *Batman/Houdini: The Devil's Workshop* (with Chaykin), *Under a Yellow Sun: A Novel by Clark Kent* from DC Comics; *Doom 2099, X-Men 2099, X-Men Unlimited, X-Factor* from Marvel Comics. TV series work includes Executive Story Consultant for *The Flash* (with Chaykin) and writing episodes of *Human Target, The Palace Guard* (with Chaykin), and *Viper*.

Question: What do you feel is one of the most critical areas on which a new writer should focus?

Beyond the formal constraints of comic storytelling—beyond format and the presentational structure—there's a great need in comics (and this applies to both writers and artists) for basic storytelling. One of the most beneficial workshops I've taken was Robert McKee's screenwriting workshop. It didn't deal with the specifics of how to write a screenplay, but was instead about how to approach telling a story. The overriding message of that seminar was before you worry about structure, know your story. Then you can fit your story into the specific format, as opposed to trying to write a story to fit the format. That is really important both for artists and writers, since both are working in service of the story. Telling a story that moves in the most articulate way possible—both visually and prosaically—is critical. Thinking about storytelling can't help but improve the quality of the work for both writers and artists. New writers and artists probably need storytelling skills the most.

THE WRITING WORK

It goes without saying that before you can send out samples of your work to a company, you must first actually do the work. Sound simplistic? Well, for a lot of aspiring professionals this can be a true revelation. Many newcomers believe that the work is only completed once the "idea" has been approved or accepted by a publisher. Not so. While it is true that many comic scripts are contracted based on proposals or plots submitted to the editor or publisher, that method of acquiring work is only used once the professional has proven his or her ability to actually produce a viable script.

A writer must create an outline or plot for a story idea, develop that idea into a full-blown story, then produce a script of the story. The script must follow a specified format considered acceptable by a particular comic company or by the comic industry as a whole. Not every company will want to see the same style of script or every step of the process taken to get there. Regardless of what the company is interested in receiving, to ensure solid story/script construction, all stages are necessary for a writer starting out.

HOW YOU CREATE YOUR WORK

Before we discuss the formatting of script, it's important to start at the very beginning of writing for comics—the methods you can use to create your work.

Until recently, the most high-tech method for writing was the typewriter, which only became popular with writers within the last 75 years. Before that it was handwriting. Plain and simple. To this day, regardless of the advent of computer technology, handwriting your work is still the easiest, most inexpensive, and most portable method. A good writer should always carry a small notebook—or at the very least a pen or pencil—with which to make quick notes when caught up in a brainstorm or moment of inspiration. And so it follows that an aspiring professional writer always ensures that they have sufficient supplies on hand and adequate work space for producing their work.

It is critical to remember, though, that a handwritten submission IS NOT acceptable for the comic industry. In order to be considered a professional it is important that your work has a professional look. All written submissions must be typed on clean, white paper stock. Publishers are not interested in specialty papers, calligraphic embellishments or your accompanying illustrations (unless you are also pursuing work as an artist). Creating your work in handwritten form is fine for your preliminary drafts, but when it's

Dave Gibbons, Writer/Artist
Credits Include: *The Watchmen* (artist), *World's Finest* (writer),
Superman: Kal (writer) with Jose Luis Garcia-Lopez for DC Comics;
Rogue Trooper (writer) with Will Simpson for Fleetway Comics and
Tundra; *Give Me Liberty* (artist), *Aliens: Salvation* (writer) with
Mike Mignola, *Martha Washington Goes to War* (artist), *Martha
Washington Saves the World* for Dark Horse Comics.

Question: When you critique a new writer's work, what are some of
the things you focus on and what type of behavior or etiquette do
you expect from them?

In a good script, every picture has a point, either to advance the plot, show
action, express character, or whatever. Space is too limited to just let things
happen, as in life. I'm also wary of huge, rambling lists of characters, locations
and events. Building a world is not the same thing as telling a story. Lastly, I
like to see clearly
differentiated characters
who speak with their
own voice.

I don't expect any
special behavior from
the recipient of my
critique, although it
seems to be almost a
rule of thumb that the
most talented are the
most courteous.
"Attitude" is best saved
for the work.

*Gibbons' art from
Martha Washington
Saves the World*

time to make a submission to a publisher, your work MUST be typed. If it is not economically feasible for you to purchase a typewriter or computer, there are a number of avenues still open to you. Ask a friend or teacher who owns a typewriter if you may use theirs. You can also avail yourself of the rental time offered by some office/copy companies (i.e., Kinkos). Your local public library or college library may have typewriters or computers available for your use. Sometimes local high schools will also offer typewriter/computer arrangements.

Just remember; a professional, typed submission will improve your chances of getting work.

Work Space

To start off, and most importantly, a writer should set aside a specific place for their writing activities. Some writers prefer to write in a quiet place. It could be a corner of their home, such as the kitchen table late at night, a small desk in their bedroom, the back porch in the early morning, or a small office set up in a spare bedroom. It could even be a quiet park bench, the local library, or a clearing in the woods. Other writers prefer to create amidst the hustle and bustle of life: a train station, an airport, a coffee shop, the shopping mall, etc. Only you, the writer, knows which setting is most effective for producing your work.

Regardless of your choice, select a location, and commit to using that place as your writing space. Only by creating a regular work setting will you be able to reliably produce work. It is important, though, to ensure that whichever location you choose, you will be able to work without distraction or interruption. These problems will only serve to hinder your chances at completing work and pursuing your chosen profession. For the purposes of simplicity, and because it is the type of work space I prefer, I will make all future references to an office area.

Invest in technology: get a good computer, a decent printer, a fax machine, and an answering machine. Your writing life will be much simpler.

TOM MASON
Co-founder, MainBrain Productions

Writing Materials

Once a writer has defined his or her work space, the next step is to acquire the materials necessary to produce the work.

If you opt for the simplest, most economical method of writing, you will be considering that tried and true system of handwritten work. You should be stocking up on writing tools (pens or pencils), paper (loose-leaf, notebooks, legal pads), and correction tools (erasers or whiteout). You should never start work without ensuring that you have sufficient materials to continue working once you are underway. Nothing is more detrimental to the creative process than an unexpected interruption to track down supplies. When your handwritten drafts are completed, always remember to have the final version typed before submission.

If you elect to use a typewriter to produce your work, be sure to keep your typing supplies fully stocked. Paper, whiteout, ribbons, erasers—all these materials are essential to an uninterrupted work flow.

If you use a computer or word processor, then make sure that you have sufficient hard-drive or disc space, and paper for the printer.

To help yourself stay organized, create a supply checklist. Run through the list before you sit down to work—much as a pilot runs through his or her start-up checklist—to make sure you're ready to go. In this way you will better track your supply needs and ensure that you are able to work without a hitch.

Reference Books

Every good writer should have one crucial reference book nearby at all times: a dictionary.

Your dictionary can be a small, inexpensive pocket dictionary, or you can splurge and invest in a larger, more comprehensive version. No matter what your choice, you should always have a dictionary handy while writing. Your dictionary will provide you with a means to spell-check your work (for those of you not using computer software). It can act as a thesaurus, if you do not have one handy. Some dictionaries also include small illustrations that can also be helpful for reference. A dictionary can even offer a great source of inspiration if you hit a dry spot in your writing. Opening the book to randomly chosen pages and

---

TOOLS FOR GOOD WRITING: REFERENCE BOOKS

Here is a list of types of reference books you should consider for use when writing. Many are available in CD-ROM format as well:

☐ Dictionary   ☐ Literature Guide

☐ Thesaurus   ☐ Dictionary of Symbolism

☐ Guide to Good Grammar   ☐ Books of Poetry

☐ Naming Dictionary   ☐ Dictionary of Word Origins

☐ Reverse Dictionary   ☐ Library Desk Reference

☐ A Dictionary of Quotations   ☐ Visual Dictionary

☐ Encyclopedias   ☐ Writing Texts

☐ Dictionary of Cultural Literacy   ☐ Science and Social Texts

---

reading a few words is a proven technique for revitalizing your creative juices, and one purportedly used by the late, great Anthony Burgess, author of *A Clockwork Orange.*

Other reference books that can be vastly helpful, and should be seriously considered as writing tools, include a thesaurus and a guide to good grammar. Both of these offer quick solutions to common writing problems, and can quickly answer questions that might interfere with the smooth flow of your writing process.

Additional reference books can be added at your discretion, depending on your writing style, interests, and abilities. You should decide which reference materials will assist you when you write, and add them as your finances will allow. Scour discount and used bookstores—a dogeared copy of a great reference book works just as well as a newly published version. Oh, and don't forget about using your local public library— always an excellent source of reference and research material.

Write.

I'm reminded of writer/artist Dave Sim at conventions with aspiring artists. They come up to him with two or three pages of storytelling art and Dave looks at that stuff, and then at the artist and says, "Now when you've done 500 of those, you'll be ready to publish."

I guess I feel the same way about writing. People have got to pay their dues and hone their craft, until they reach the point where their work is, in fact, publishable. As with anything, writing is a learning process. You might start out being sort of okay, or not okay, but the more you practice, the better you're going to get, if you're determined. With writing, if you wait for the muse to hit, you might be waiting for the rest of your life. You have to sit in front of your typewriter or computer for a specified number of hours every day. You don't wait for inspiration. You've got to sit there and force yourself to write. Some days you're going to come away with nothing of value—your garbage can is going to be full. But if you keep at it, you're eventually going to walk away with stuff you can use, work you can publish. Work that's worthy of being published. But you have got to make yourself sit down and do it. And do it. And do it. Until you're good enough at it, so that eventually your garbage can is less full at the end of the day.

DIANA SCHUTZ
Editor-in-Chief for Dark Horse Comics

Your Writing Skills

If you have never had any training or education for writing skills, then it's a good idea to get some before getting started. That's not to say that you don't already have the skills necessary to be a successful writer or that all published comic professionals have an educational background in writing. However, if your writing skills are rough edged—or worse, amateurish—then you should seriously consider learning some of the basics before you get started writing comics.

There is a vast assortment of places a writer can go to get an education. It can be as complex as getting a writing degree in English literature or journalism at a university, for

Diana Schutz, Editor-in-Chief for Dark Horse Comics
Credits Include: *Grendel, Mage, Johnny Quest, Rio, Batman/Grendel, Night and the Enemy* (with Harlan Ellison) from Comico; *Grendel, Rio, American Splendor,* a variety of Eddie Campbell books, *Batman/Predator, The Jam* from Dark Horse.

Question: Which style of scripting do you prefer to use?

As an editor working on scripts, either plot-style or full-style scripting is fine. I think plot-style tends to encourage more participation on the part of the artist, but really the bottom line is the writer's attitude toward his or her script—how proprietary he or she is. The most important thing for me is that no matter what style of script is used, once the pencils are done I like to send those to the writers, in order for them to revise the script if necessary. It seems a given that the artist will visualize the script differently than the writer did when he or she was writing it. I think it's very important at that point to make the collaboration as seamless as possible. It's important for the writer to be able to go back and take another look at the script since the artwork may now suggest new things, or make other things from the original script redundant, and the writer needs to basically accommodate the script to the artwork. Again, all in the spirit of collaboration. In my view, this tends to make for a more tightly knit story.

For an unsolicited submission, in general, there is no preference for the type of scripting submitted. However, I would say it's probably better for a writer to do a full-style script. Generally, if people can write full-style scripts they can also write plot-style. The reverse is not always true. Certainly in order to show an editor that you, as a writer, are comfortable with the mechanics, visuals, pacing, composition, etc. of comics, you're probably better off sending in a full-style script. However, I will add that our submissions editor certainly does not want to see a full 24-page script! But he would want to see a full-style sample of scripting.

example, or as simple as picking up some instructional books and practicing your art (see Appendix C for more information on improving your writing skills). Whichever path you choose, just be sure you have a working knowledge of basics of writing before you endeavor to join the profession. Lapses in the basics like grammar, spelling, and format can seriously interfere with your chances of acquiring work in the comics industry. Many editors and publishers you will approach come from a literary background or have some degree of professional experience with writing. The flaws in your writing skills will be glaringly obvious to them, and if they believe you lack the basic skills necessary to write professionally your chances of getting work are severely diminished.

As an occasional writer, I tend to use a kind of hybrid scripting style. I will designate a particular page, or group of pages, describe all the action that is occurring on those pages—even if the "action" is entirely psychological as opposed to physical—and then will write in the narrative captions and dialogue. This allows the artist more control, but at the same time gives him or her an awareness of what the characters will be saying, thinking, and so on. But it also leaves to the artist's discretion such things as pacing, for example, or at least allows the artist to contribute more in the area of pacing. This type of scripting makes for a more collaborative effort, which I feel unless you're a single writer/artist—should be as seamless as possible. This [type of scripting] seems a good way of achieving that collaboration, because the comic artist is as involved as the writer in telling the story. This is as opposed to prose illustration, when the story is already done and the illustrations are almost adjuncts. The illustrations are very pretty, but not required for the story to be told. With comics, one of the defining characteristics of the best examples of the medium is when the words and pictures are interdependent—the one cannot function without the other.

HOW TO GET STARTED

Getting a Story Idea

The question writers most often hear (and dread) is, "Where do you get your ideas?"

The answer is not a simple one. Much has been written by authors in all literary fields about this subject, and every answer is a little different. What it all boils down to is that each writer comes up with ideas in his or her own unique way. I will assume that since you are reading this book, you are an aspiring writer who has a rash of ideas that you are just dying to put to paper. Therefore, this question is of little import for you, right?

Wrong.

Many aspiring writers have a rash of new ideas, true enough. But often that's exactly where it ends—with that one batch of ideas. Soon an aspiring writer has "used up" those ideas, by putting them to paper, and is dismayed to find they've all been rejected by the target publishers. So, does this mean that they were never meant to be writers? Possibly. But if you are convinced that this is what you want to do for a living, then get serious about your career. This means it is time to cultivate new ideas.

There are loads of reference and self-improvement books that can offer you information on how to get your creative juices going. They all have great suggestions, but my personal favorite, and probably the simplest, is: read. Yes, it is as simple as that. Read. Read a lot. Read fiction, read nonfiction, read magazines, read signs, read billboards, read the telephone book, read *TV Guide,* read graffiti. Read anything you can get your "Vulcan-squinties" on. Because reading opens up your mind, gives you pause, triggers thoughts, fantasies, ideas. Yes, ideas. And that's where you want to start, with an idea.

Now, what happens if you're one of those folks who has more good ideas than time to write them into stories? Or what if your ideas are just disembodied concepts, descriptions, or inventions? Then you need a file or record for your ideas. Some authors keep notebooks, others use file cards (like me), and some just scribble on scraps of paper and throw them in file folders or drawers. You need to choose a system that will work well for you. Keep a log of your ideas. Try to organize them into categories, stories, costumes, characters, premises, etc. Then, if you're at a creative impasse, you can simply read your idea file. This process will make a world of difference in your creative production.

The Plot and Outline

To begin with, what exactly are "the plot" and "the outline?"

The most common definition of plot is everything that happens in a story. On a more technical level, a plot is built of significant events, with important consequences, that comprise the story. It is the things characters do, feel, think, or say that influence the outcome of the story. Plotting is a way of deciding what's important in a story, then showing it to be important through the way you construct and connect the major events in your story. A plot is your idea developed into a story (see boxed example on page 36).

The outline could be considered the skeletal structure on which your story hangs. It is the "bare bones" version of the story. The outline is generally used to propose a story to a potential publisher. A well-constructed outline covers all aspects of your story, and is a brief description of the plot, subplot, action, and character interaction. It takes the form of a story describing everything from the idea on through each and every scene. All key characters are described, their relationships to and with one another, and the ways and means by which the action proceeds. An outline can also be vastly helpful in the actual writing process, providing the author with a clear and stable structure on which to build the details of the story (see boxed example on page 37).

In the comic industry, the plot is often confused with the outline. Some companies use a scripting format they like to call "plotting" or "the plot." This simply consists of a

Jerry Prosser, Writer

Credits Include: *Exquisite Corpse, Aliens: Hive, Cyberantics,* and *Predator: Invaders from the Fourth Dimension* from Dark Horse Comics; *Skin Graft: Adventures of a Tattooed Man* and *Animal Man* from DC/Vertigo; Bram Stoker's *Burial of the Rats* from Cosmic.

Question: Of the many different types of story proposals (i.e., regular series, one-shots, mini-series, etc.), which do you believe have the best chance of being considered, and why?

I really think the best thing is a fill-in for a regular series—perhaps one or two issues.

That's the likeliest kind of proposal an editor is going to be able to evaluate. They're always going to need fill-in material, simply because of the rigors of a monthly book schedule. I also think short stories, for an anthology-style book, are really good, although they tend to sell faster and easier, if an artist is already attached to the project. It's not essential, but it really does help—especially if you're sending in a story cold. Always keep in mind that for almost any editor, looking at unsolicited submissions is probably their lowest work priority—especially writing submissions. It takes a long time for them to reply and even a really good proposal doesn't guarantee that the writer can do the work.

I think the biggest issue with trying to break into the comics business as a writer is that it's much more difficult for an editor to evaluate a writer's work quickly, than it is to evaluate an artist's work. So I think the more you can associate yourself with visual material the easier the sell is going to be. With that in mind, keeping your submission brief—a one-page summary and some sample scripting—is the way it has to be.

A submission that features an original, creator-owned project is going to have a slimmer chance at being considered, unless it's something that can be pitched for an anthology that's specially geared for that kind of material. As a previously un-published writer your chances of getting a new series looked at are very slim.

Finally, nothing shows an editor that a prospective writer can do the job better than to actually see published work. So if it's at all possible for an aspiring writer to make his or her own mini-comics or self-publish something—even if it's a very small run—I think it can be a very powerful sales tool.

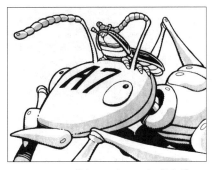

Cyberantics *art by Rick Geary*

Bernie 2000
"Miss Venus Beach"
Plot for an 8-page story
October 16, 1999

Lurene Haines
123 My Street
This Town, FL 32500

Miss Venus Beach

Bernie is to judge the Miss Venus Beach Contest. All Shoreside girls are dying to enter and win the big "mystery prize." Victoria is completely confident she'll win, and spends most of the week prior shopping at the most exclusive shops for body paints, sexy suits...even the latest expensive toy—a holo-backdrop to best complement her look. At the last minute, she decides to give out travel tips (which would only apply to the wealthy, of course) as her talent segment. Peggy decides to take another tack. With inside info that Bernie's parents are on vacation, and that he's been fending for himself for meals, Peggy goes for simple good looks, and concentrates her time on making a gourmet meal for the talent portion. On the day of the contest, Bernie spends most of his time ogling Victoria and eating Peggy's food. In the end though, Victoria wins. The big "mystery prize" is revealed—a date with Bernie! Peggy gets the last laugh though, since, as always, Bernie is broke.

Example of a plot

page-by-page outline of the comic story. As we can see by the above descriptions, the plot is merely the encapsulated version of the overall story, and is generally no more than a single paragraph in length. The outline expands on the plot, fleshing out specific characters and events, and how they will interact and transpire in greater detail. The outline can be anywhere from one to three pages long. Don't let the terminology confuse you as a newcomer. When in doubt, ask the editor to elaborate.

Scripting

This is the discussion for which many of you have been anxiously waiting—scripting: what is it, why it is needed, how to do it, and proper format.

Scripting for the comic industry is similar to the type of scripting done for television and film. Though the storytelling method in comics tends to parallel that of the visual

Lurene Haines   December 14, 1999
123 My Street   Copyright © 1999 Lurene Haines
This Town, FL 32500

<u>In These Blue Depths Lie Hell: A Proposal for a 15-Page Story</u>

An angry storm whips the Straits of Florida. The year is 1528, and the crew of the galleon, Fuerza de Dios, are engaged in a fierce battle with the soldiers of Hell—called forth by the very man who was to provide them with God's protection and blessings. In present time, a similar, although much more subtle, battle of good and evil has also begun. Entwining a triangle of unknowing lovers who holiday in the Florida Keys, it is about to consume the man who is the direct descendent of Eduardo Protegera, captain of the doomed Fuerza de Dios.

Husband and wife, Tony and Claire, have brought their close friend Nerissa on holiday with them. Two of them are lovers. One plans the untimely demise of the third. The other acquiesces reluctantly, and a diving expedition to an ancient shipwreck is secretly designated as the killing field.

Padre de Bogado was just a man...with evil tastes. His compulsion to solve the mysteries of the ancient manuscript was a hot, burning secret he laid with every night. The voyage to the New World presented him with the time to find the answers...and bring a culmination to the exquisite tortures he so fiercely desired. How could he have known of the fate he called upon the men of the Fuerza de Dios...or did he knowingly embrace their sacrifice when he called the demons. Captain Protegera proves the only one capable of stopping the actions of Hell itself. But it is only an eternity in frozen battle with Evil, while both wait for help from a distant future.

The three divers discover the submerged hulk of the chain-wrapped ship as the ancient maps promised. And it is here that the lovers, Nerissa and Clare, choose to kill Tony. But as the knife is raised and the struggle commences, a hand from Hell reaches from the wreckage and wrenches the three divers into a hideous limbo where a much more desperate battle has resumed. There, Tony is stunned by the presence of his ancestor, who entreats him to aid in the destruction of the ship. Meanwhile, the demon hopes to enlist the aid of the two women. Unfortunately, they are ineffective in their shock, and grisly punishments are doled out. Meanwhile, Tony and Eduardo manage to achieve the massive explosion they need to destroy the ship. Although it appears they have won, and Tony bursts from the surface of the ocean free of the past and the battle, Hell is not to be denied, and sends one last chain to hook the soul that almost got away.

Example of an outline

electronic mediums, it is still a unique storytelling form. TV, movies, and comics do have one major characteristic in common: The storytelling occurs in both words and pictures. However, in comics, there is no live action or continuous flow of movement to advance events. The script must be carefully and masterfully constructed to reveal the story through a series of pictures, on a series of pages, sometimes continuing through a series of issues or books. This type of storytelling requires a skillful writer who is able to integrate the words of the story with the visual images, and maximize the use of the page image as a whole. (For more information on the art of comic storytelling, see Appendix C.)

As a rule, in the comic industry, a script is the fully written text of a comic book story. It is laid out in such a manner as to describe the story elements—plot, character, action—and tell the story from beginning to end detailing both the visual and text aspects of the story. Simply put, a comic script describes the images or action you will see, and the words you will read that accompany those images.

ProFile

John Ostrander, Freelance Writer
Credits Include: *Suicide Squad* (with Kim Yale), *Wasteland*, *Firestorm*, *The Specter*, *Gotham Nights II* from DC Comics; *Magnus Robot Fighter*, *Rai*, *Eternal Warrior* from Valiant; *Elf Quest: Jink* from Warp Graphics; *Grimjack* from First Comics; *Bishop* mini-series, *Wolverine* graphic novel (with Tom Mandrake) from Marvel Comics.

Question: What business tactics would you recommend to help newcomers avoid being "pigeon-holed" creatively?

This reminds me of the actors I worked with back when I was an acting coach in Chicago. There were actors who were concerned about being typecast. My advice to them was "Get hired a lot first, then worry about being typecast." This advice applies to comics also. For newcomers, I think the basic concern is getting hired in the first place, not getting pigeon-holed.

I think it's more constructive to ask them, "What kind of work is it that you really want to do?" If they don't want to do superheroes, then they shouldn't start off doing superheroes. On the other hand, it's tougher to get your start that way in this field, particularly if you want to make a living at it. The bulk of the work that's available in comics and with the major companies, is superhero work. So, if you can do that or are interested in that, then that's fine. If it's not what you do, or not what you do well, then be honest with yourself and don't do it.

Although there are some companies in the comic industry that prefer to work from an outline of the story, most companies require a full script—or at least proof that you can write a full script. The script serves as the guiding tool for the art team assigned to the project. Your story must be realized in a visual form to classify as a comic book, and the script is the tool by which the artists interpret your story. Additionally, since most comic book projects are a team effort, the script provides the team with an indisputable reference point. The editor can use the script to guide each member of the creative team, hopefully producing a successful and skillfully done finished product.

Until you have established yourself as a solid, proven professional, it is unlikely that you will be permitted to produce work without completing a script of some type. If you are a writer/artist creating art for your own story, you may be given slightly more latitude on the written end, but you will still be required to produce some sort of "script" (even if it's rough sketches or thumbnails of the action) for the publisher to approve.

Some newcomers come up to me and ask, "What's the secret formula for writing a script?"

I tell them simply, "There is no secret." There are two ways you can write a script; the traditional way [full-style] and the Marvel way [plot-style]. So long as you can tell which panel is which, and who's saying what, that's pretty much it. You don't have to worry about things like what size an indention you should use. People are often very concerned with the format, which I don't think is relevant at all.

STEVE ENGLEHART
Writer

Script Format

Regardless of the style of scripting you choose, there are a number of required basic format items that remain unchanged. Margins, spacing, titles, headers, capitalization—these items are relatively consistent between scripting styles. Here's a rundown of the basics.

1. **Margins:** Be generous. Allow at least 1" of margin all the way around. Leave an additional 1/4" at the top of each page for header placement. Extra margin space can be useful to an editor who wishes to make notes, so don't skimp. Also, you should start the first page of your script with extra space at the top to allow for the title.

2. **Title:** Unlike video or film scripts, a comic script does not necessarily require a title page. Place the title on the first page of the script, at the top. Be sure to include your name, contact information, the date, and a copyright notice if you own the material. You can also include the total page count for the comic story and a brief description of the contents (i.e., a three-issue mini-series). The title information can either be centered or divided and placed flush left and right.

3. **Page Headers:** Every page of your script should have a header. The name of the script story and your last name should be flush to the left. The page number of the

script should be flush to the right. Another acceptable style of header places the title of the work at the right with the page number.

4. **Spacing:** Double space between different character's word balloon dialogue, between dialogue and captions, between dialogue or captions and sound effects, and between panel descriptions and dialogue. Single space for lines of panel description and within each individual block of dialogue or caption text.

5. **Capitalization:** When typing your script, specific items must be capitalized for clarity's sake. In general, the following elements are in all caps: caption labels, sound effects, and character names (full-style script: capitalize dialogue name labels only; plot-style script: capitalize names in the body of the page descriptions).

I" MARGINS
ALL AROUND

NAME AND CONTACT
INFO ON FIRST PAGE

TITLE

NAME OF PROJECT AND
PAGE NUMBER ON EVERY PAGE

Lurene Haines
123 My Street
Thistown, FL 32000
(123) 456-7890

Angelus/Decay - Page 1 of 1

Angelus, Part 1: Decay

One Page--Six panels. Banner across top: angelus: decay, story and art by lurene haines

Panel 1: Full bleed running the vertical height of the page. Establishing shot of Angelus. Leaning or lying, head tipped back slightly and to one side-toward story. This shows the detail of Angelus' costume. Add good BG details: plants, ribbons. Make sure to show the angel wings on the palm of her black hand.

Panel 2: Long shot, full figure of Angelus standing in the middle of a black-and-white checkered tile floor. Angelus is looking into an ornate hand mirror she holds.

A1: Decay is a required condition of Life.
A2: It invades all aspects of humanity: Virtue. Chastity. Relationships. Faith. Hope. Power. Innocence. However these forms of Decay are accepted, expected, sometimes embraced; but never shrouded in the very public fear

PANEL DESCRIPTION—
DOUBLE SPACE BETWEEN PANELS

DIALOGUE AND CAPTIONS:
• INDENT FROM PANEL DESCRIPTION
• LABEL WITH CHARACTER NAMES
• NUMBER EACH WORD BALLOON

Suggested structure for a script

Kelley Puckett, Writer
Credits Include: *Green Arrow, Batman Adventures, Superman &*
Batman for DC Comics.

Question: What business tactics would you recommend to help
newcomers avoid being "pigeon-holed" creatively?

Diversify. Work with as many different companies and editors as you possibly
can. Having a lot of different contacts not only makes you seem more "in
demand," but also suggests that you have some creative range. The only person
who can keep you from being "pigeon-holed," however, is you. Do your best
to keep switching gears. If you got your start on an obsessed loner vigilante
project, actively seek out work that's very different: a group book, a funny
animal book, whatever.
And be on the lookout for
the early warning signs of
being "pegged." If you get
a call from someone who
says they really enjoyed
your work on Rodent-Man
and they've got a project
for you that's "just like it,"
it's time to start worrying.

*Art from
The Batman
Adventures*

Comparing Company Scripts

In the comic industry the format of the script varies widely between companies—and sometimes even within a company. Some publishers will tell you in no uncertain terms that they will only accept a particular script format or will absolutely refuse to consider another scripting form; other companies are much more flexible in their requirements; and some are only interested in plots, not scripts. To ensure that you are submitting the correct format, or at the very least one that will be considered favorably, it is in your best professional interest to send for the target company's submission guidelines. Most companies will offer a sample page of script format considered acceptable by that company on request. Ensure you adhere to the accepted form for each company, when you send out samples, if you hope to be considered.

There are currently two main scripting forms used in the comic industry. There are a plethora of other related forms, and you are free to adapt the scripting format to fit your preferences, but it is always important to remember that simplicity works best.

Write from the heart. Don't contrive plots for some perceived audience, unless you are doing work-for-hire for some perceived audience.

DENIS KITCHEN
Publisher, Kitchen Sink Press, Inc.

The Full-Style Script

Many companies, including DC Comics, prefer to use a full-style script. These scripts are laid out as if the action were to occur on film or stage. The descriptions can include action descriptions (panel by panel) or scene descriptions (page by page). The characters are described in detail, and all dialogue, captions and sound effects are included.

These scripts are completed prior to release to the art team to provide them with a solidly structured story on which to build the images. The art team will have some latitude to interpret the descriptions and actions, but in general is required to adhere to the script contents and has little say in the story dialogue.

Within the full-style script there are many variations in format. Consistencies lie in the way the story is broken down and laid out. (See box on page 43 for an example of a full-style comic script.) Here are some general guidelines:

1. **Page:** In general, each page of the comic book is described separately. Most times each new comic page begins with a fresh script page. If the script for a single comic page runs longer than one script page, it is formally continued on the next page.

2. **Panel:** Each panel of the comic page should be described. The action, the setting, the characters are all included in the panel description. This is also where the dialogue and captions are written.

3. **Dialogue and Captions:** When writing the dialogue and captions in a full-style script, each item must be identified. If one character will speak three times in a single panel (i.e., three word balloons), then that character's dialogue must be broken down as three parts. Each time a separate caption or word balloon occurs, it must be clearly labeled.

NEBULA BATTLES Issue #2—"Duel On Vena Blahaad"
Script version 9.1.99 By Joe Writer

* * *

Two panels.

1. <u>BIG PANEL</u>. The STAR HAWK coming in over the spaceport Vena Blahaad. We're farther out than the shot in NB #1/page 4, giving us a more extensive view of the "horizon to horizon" spaceport city.

A single great <u>World Eater</u> is sitting in low orbit over the Rayetta sector. The "ship monitoring buoy" that will <u>pierce</u> this World Eater on page 24 is visible in the shot—this "SMB" is a corroded chrome-green metallic circular structure, that rises above the sector. The structure's apex is domed and pointed, encircled with large view-ports. It is here that <u>Danish Daksh</u> keeps an eye on all traffic entering and leaving the Rayetta Sector.

The great planet Benj Witek is in the background—perhaps making a huge crescent at top of page?

    <u>CAPTION</u>: Cam and Isobel return to the spaceport moon Vena Blahaad, where Cam learned the runner's trade as a youth—and where Isobel was given an ancient energybow by an old woman Gunda named Jametta Lo-Fendi!

    <u>CAM</u> (balloon from Hawk): <u>World Eater—over the Rayetta sector!</u>

    <u>CAM</u> (linked): Just our luck!

2. Wide panel. (Could be an inset into panel 1, which can be a full-pager.)

The traditional head-on view of the Hawk cockpit, showing all the crew and passengers: VAZUL and CAM at the controls. ISOBEL and BALTA ZTANG behind CAM. . . JAVE SEVRA behind VAZUL,

    <u>ISOBEL:</u> The Star Hawk is a priority Dynasty quarry—

    <u>CAM:</u> Yea—and their scanners are tracking our approach right now!

    <u>VAZUL:</u> Screehaaan!

    <u>BALTA:</u> Give me the helm, Cam! I know a secret route through the old Aneurin sector.

Example of full-style scripting

The Plot-Style Script

A number of companies, including Marvel Comics, prefer to work with a plot-style script. In these scripts, the action, individual pages, or comic book as a whole, are described in outline form. These outlines are then given to the artistic team for interpretation. Once the art has been roughed in with each page designed and the panels of action laid out, the writer is given copies, and proceeds to complete the finished scripting with dialogue and captions.

As with the full-style scripts, there is much variation in the format of the plot-style scripts. Some writers and editors prefer to work with a much looser structured story to give the artistic team a lot of creative freedom. Others prefer a more tightly structured plot, and essentially leave only panel design to the creative team. (See box on page 45 for an example of a plot-style comic script.) Here are some general guidelines:

1. **Page:** In general, plot-style scripts stick to page descriptions and tend to skip panel-by-panel breakdowns. For this reason, it is not required that each page of the comic book begin on a fresh script page. Each comic page is labeled and includes a brief description of the characters, action, and setting. In some situations, a writer will also include dialogue, but often this is left for a later stage in the production.

2. **Dialogue and Captions:** If the script is done in true plot-style form, the dialogue and captions are written, for the most part, after the rough art has been done based on the original plot-style script. Once the roughs are completed the writer is given a copy and proceeds to write the character dialogue and captions. Sometimes these are written at the same time as the plotting is done. This tends to vary depending on the individual company or editor.

The Pros and Cons: A Comparison of Scripting Styles

Since there is no single accepted scripting format in the comics industry, it has become a source of much heated debate. Depending on personal preferences, company loyalties, or experience, many professionals argue staunchly for one scripting format over another.

Full-style proponents tend to argue that this scripting style ensures that the original vision is more truly interpreted by the artistic team. Editors and publishers often prefer this script style because it ensures that the writing work is completed before the next stage of the project gets underway and gives them a solid structure on which to build the art, and a reliable reference point. Opponents of this style argue that it can restrict creativity.

Supporters of the plot-style scripting state that it encourages the creative process, and results in a more integrated team effort. Editors and publishers like the fact that the basic structure is in place for the story, but the artistic team is able to take a freer hand with the interpretation. Opponents argue that the final results are often vastly divergent from the original concept, in other words, too many cooks spoil the broth!

Despite the different styles in scripting, the most important thing to remember is that before submitting work to a company you should be familiar with their submission requirements. There is little point in actively soliciting work from a company that prefers the full-style script by submitting plot-style scripts, or vice versa.

LETHOS #7 "Variations on a Scream"   Jane Scribe
Plot for 24 pages   12/31/99

PAGE ONE/SPLASH PAGE:

OPEN ON: a scene straight out of a Hollywood monster film, with the charismatic, darkly cloaked vampire clutching a swooning woman in a gauzy white low-cut gown, about to plunge his fangs into her delicate throat. The catch here is that the woman is ALTHEA RONICE (from issue 1) and the vampire is LETHOS.

PAGE TWO:

LETHOS sinks his teeth into ALTHEA'S neck; she gasps and swoons in the usual style of the romanticized vampire's victims. She clutches his head closer to her neck, "Emanuel. . . my love," she whispers passionately. LETHOS lifts his head from her neck, tiny drops of ruby-colored blood at the corners of his mouth. "Althea, my darling," he says, "you and I shall be together forever—our love shall transcend mortality." LETHOS pulls his silken shirt open and bares his neck to her. "Drink of my blood," he says, "so that you may be immortal with me."

PAGE THREE:

ALTHEA lifts her head toward LETHOS, kissing him. In a flurry of heated kisses, she moves toward his throat. SUDDENLY, the door of the room bursts open—WHAM! ALTHEA'S head whirls, a terror-filled expression on her face, while LETHOS turns to the intruders and snarls with righteous indignation. ANGLE ON THE DOOR as we see proper English vampire fighters—and PROFESSOR DEMETRIS, dressed as VAN HELSING—bursting into the room carrying crucifixes and wooden stakes. "Your evil dreams have come to an end, Count Lethos," DEMETRIS/VAN HELSING says.

PAGE FOUR:

LETHOS snarls and shakes a fist at DEMETRIS/VAN HELSING. "I'll see you suffer the tortures of the pit for this, Van Demetris!" DEMETRIS/VAN HELSING thrusts his crucifix at LETHOS who roars with outrage, turns, and leaps through the window, shattering it. CUT TO outside, as LETHOS lands on the chalet grounds below—just as the sun rises. "No!" he screams, "Van Demetris has tricked me!" LETHOS is destroyed by the sun's rays, turned into a smoking pile of ash. Out of the ashes, an ASTRAL FORM of LETHOS appears, as he usually looks, and streaks away from the scene. SUDDENLY, the whole landscape begins to fade away. . .

Example of plot-style scripting

Tony Isabella, Writer/Columnist
Credits Include: *Avengers, Spider-Man, Daredevil, Ghost Rider, Dracula* for Marvel; *Hawkman* and *Black Lightning* for DC Comics; *Satan's Six* for Topps; Justice Machine for Comico; regular column contributor for *Comics Buyer's Guide.*

Question: Which style of scripting do you prefer to use?

I don't have any real preference. Unless a company predetermines the style of scripting, I let myself be guided by the artist I'm working with. Generally speaking, if I am working with an artist with whom I'm not real confident, or one who prefers it, I'll go full-script style. If I've got an artist whose work I really don't like, I'll always go full-script style. That way I won't have to actually look at the artwork when I'm writing the story. But it really depends on the artist since I don't really have any preference. I let the company and/or the artist determine which method I choose to use.

Given that editors very rarely have the time to read lengthy submissions, I would suggest that if new writers intend to send a full story to an editor, that they send a page-by-page plot and a few pages of full script. This will give the editor an idea of what their actual writing style is like. If the company already has guidelines in place for script submissions, the would-be writer should follow those. If left to their own devices, they should submit an outline and maybe a few pages broken down plot-style.

In my case, there's very little difference between my panel descriptions for plot-style or full-style scripts, because I basically do a panel-by-panel plot when I do plot-style scripts. For my plot-style scripts, the first thing I do is break down the story on index cards. Then I do a panel-by-panel plot. It will have an indication of dialogue in the plot, but not the actual dialogue. There's just

enough so that the artist knows where I'm going. I figure that with a plot-style script the artist has a lot more leeway. But there are artists who want as much information as possible, so I give them a panel-by-panel breakdown, and if they want to break it down differently, they're free to do so.

Art from DC Comics' Black Lightning

Get professional training. I really recommend to people who are sincere about writing comics, including artists who want to become writers, that they try to get professional training. Although there are not a lot of courses for writing comics specifically, other training exists. Screenwriting classes, in particular, are superb. They focus on visual storytelling. Even short story writing classes are good, because the components of character development, dialogue, story pacing are all relevant to comics. People who have had some training—even if it's just a class or two—seem to be better at pitching their ideas, doing a professional presentation of their work, interacting with editors, and identifying the kinds of things that need to go into a story to satisfy an editor. There are many people with a lot of good ideas out there, who will never make it into comics writing because they haven't picked up those additional writing skills that are necessary to turn the ideas into actual, saleable stories.

LEN STRAZEWSKI
Writer

HONING YOUR SKILLS AS A WRITER

Even if you've now reached the point where you feel your writing skills are sufficient to acquire work in the comic industry, don't stop there. One of the marks of a consummate professional is to constantly strive to improve and grow as a creator. You have a responsibility to practice your craft and improve your skills throughout your career. Start now. Here are a few suggestions to get you going:

- Carefully proofread your work more than once. Also, try to have someone else read it over to help you catch mistakes.

- Take every opportunity to practice your writing.

- Don't restrict yourself to comic storytelling. Expand and try new genres and markets.

- Keep up in your technical and trade magazine reading. Constantly search out new material and information to help improve your skills.

- Take writing classes or courses that will help you develop in a related or unrelated area (e.g., study classic literature at the community college, send for a correspondence course in novel writing).

- Meet with other comic writers or fellow professionals to discuss your work and the work being published in the industry.

- Join an on-line computer discussion group focused on writing.

- Participate in a writer's workshop or retreat to work on your writing skills.

- Pay attention to the creative feedback and critiques you receive, and utilize this information for improving your writing.

Do not become a comic book writer. Become a writer who writes comic books.

MARK EVANIER
Writer

Rune #6 Dialogue script

Artist and story editor: Barry Windsor-Smith

Traffic editor: Dan Danko

Writer: Chris Ulm

<u>Draft History</u>

- Created: September 5, 1994
- Mantra/Prime Dialogue (pages 1–12), approved by Mike Barr, Len Strazeweski, September 10, 1994.

PAGE 1

Panel 1:

(1) CAP

June 1, 1994.

(2) CAP

The PALACE exudes an ancient EVIL.

(3) CAP

Once, it was the HEART of a FAR FLUNG EMPIRE....

(4) CAP

Its marble stonework consecrated by the BLOOD of NATIONS....

(5) CAP

Its hallways PAVED with plundered GOLD.

(6) CAP

Now, even in DECAY, it is a fitting LAIR for one who considers himself a DEITY...

(7) CAP

The DARK GOD....

Panel 2:

(8) CAP (large)

<u>RUNE</u>

Example of a final draft script from Rune #6, Malibu Comics. (Artwork on page 50.)

                         (9) RUNE

The MYSTIC BLADE is on this planet—yet its whereabouts
REMAIN UNCLEAR to me...

                         (10) RUNE

Seek my DESIRE, vessel—

                         (11) RUNE

Unearth the WEAPON I CRAVE...

                         (12) RUNE

FIND the SWORD OF FANGS

CREDITS

    Barry Windsor-Smith-Pencils, Editor

    Chris Ulm, Script

    Alex Bialy, Inks

    Patrick Owsley, Letters

    Rune created by Barry Windsor-Smith & Chris Ulm

PAGE 2

Panel 1

                    (1) RUNE (LARGE)

DEFY MY WILL NO LONGER!

PANEL 2

                         (2) RUNE

SHE is the one? Such a WEAPON in the hands of an ignorant
MORTAL?

                         (3) RUNE

No MATTER. What was MINE shall be MINE AGAIN!

                         (4) RUNE

SO SWEARS THE PRINCE OF VOID!

PAGE 3

Panel 1

Example of final artwork from Rune #6, Malibu Comics.

Example of a finished page from Rune #6, *Malibu Comics, Writer: Chris Ulm, Artist: Barry Windsor-Smith*

CHAPTER THREE

PREPARING YOUR SAMPLES

A writing sample is just what it sounds like—a sample of your writing work. Now, as simplistic as that might seem, there are very specific elements that are critical to properly prepared writing samples. Because of the degree of difficulty involved in breaking into the comics industry as a writer, it's critical that you use every tool and skill available to you to improve your chances of acquiring work. Your samples are one of these tools.

The only way to ensure that they provide you with the edge you need to compete in the comics market is to guarantee that you've followed acceptable form in preparing those samples. Improperly prepared samples are generally rejected out-of-hand. This chapter is designed to show you the way to correctly prepare your samples, and thus increase your advantage.

A COMIC INDUSTRY ASIDE

If you're dedicated to the idea of writing exclusively for the comic industry, it'll pay to keep in mind the parameters of comic storytelling. You must tailor your concepts and ideas to the industry in which you hope to publish.

For example, today's comic industry has little interest in pulp-romance comics. If you are only interested in producing formula pulp-romance stories, you are likely to encounter a world of problems getting published. That's not to say that there isn't a market available for that genre. If you are a good writer, you will be able to tailor your subject of interest to the form accepted by your target publisher. For example, if you can create a fascinating, well-written pulp-romance story that works well within a superhero context, then you have a much better chance of being considered by DC Comics or Marvel Comics.

For this reason, it is important to tailor your ideas to the industry. Don't curb your creative processes, or throw out a good idea just because you're sure it won't fit. File it away. As you gain writing experience you may find a couple of things will happen: One, adapting your previously unacceptable idea will be a much more effortless task than when you started out; or, two, you might develop an interest in another literary area or genre where that idea can be used.

Read everything—especially stuff that's not comics. The biggest problem with writers today is that all they know is comic books, so there aren't many new ideas being generated. Mostly all they're doing is recycling stories that have already been told. The reason Frank Miller and Alan Moore are such brilliant writers is because they have brought so many outside influences into their comic writing.

SCOTT PETERSON
Editor, Batman Group Liaison, DC Comics

THE STRUCTURE OF A GOOD SAMPLE

Keep in mind that most publishers and editors are generally overworked, inundated with distractions, and struggling to make their own careers run smoothly. It's obvious that it is in your best interest to make the process of considering your writing samples the smoothest and easiest possible. If you make considering your work essentially effortless, then your chances of having your samples looked at are greatly increased. There are plenty of gimmicks and tricks that will get you noticed. But being noticed doesn't always guarantee that your work will be read. The goal here is to get the editor to look at your work, then you have a chance to hook them and perhaps they'll read more.

The first and most important characteristic of your samples should be brevity. More is not always better. You must remember that the editor who reads your work is on a very tight schedule. The opportunities to read new, unsolicited submissions are few and far between. Keep your first page of samples short and to the point. DO NOT send a full script as an unsolicited submission. Aside from the fact that most editors won't read a full script due to liability factors (i.e., fear that the company will be accused of stealing the story), they just don't have the time to read all that material. On the other hand, make sure your samples are complete. Don't skimp on the content in the interest of keeping your samples brief. Learn to reach a balance in the content: just the right amount to hook the reader, and whet their appetite for more, but not so much that they can't wait to dispose of your package.

With brevity in mind, your sample should be composed of three basic parts: a cover letter, a proposal or outline, and samples of scripting. Each of these sections should be concise, to the point, and thoroughly businesslike. Additionally, your total sample package should not exceed five pages.

The Cover Letter

Except when handing your work to a professional in person, your samples should always be accompanied by a cover letter. The cover letter gives you a chance to briefly introduce yourself, outline your specific interests and goals, and detail any other writing credits you may have. There are many business texts that detail the anatomy of a good cover letter, and it would be a good idea to check out some of these books. Also, before jotting off a cover letter, take the time to experiment a bit. Compose a couple of trial letters, playing with the format and content. Then choose the cover letter that best represents you, as a writer.

Joe Pruett, Writer/Editor, Creative Director for Caliber Comics
Credits Include: *Negative Burn, Black Mist, Exit, Boneshaker* (editor);
Kilroy Is Here, Soul, and *Dance with the Gods* (creator/writer) from
Caliber Press.

Question: What elements do you feel are critical for professionally
prepared samples and, as an editor, what do you specifically look for
in a sample pack or proposal?

I look to see if a writer can successfully hook me on an idea (short story, series,
etc.) in a short, concise, and well-written paragraph. The writer must make me
want to see more. I need to feel that the characters come alive, that they have
personalities and aren't just cardboard cutouts.

There also should be a beginning, middle, and an end to each story. You'd be
surprised how often I receive boring stories in which nothing happens. The characters should change because of the circumstances that the story presents to them.
If he or she can do all of this, then they are on their way to becoming a writer.

What I look for in a submission from a writer is a good detailed proposal. I
prefer not to see full scripts unless I ask for them. Writers must remember that an
editor is extremely busy and you only have a minute to catch their eye with your
proposal. If you send in an unsolicited full script then odds are likely that the editor
will skip right over it and read the next submission on the pile from the person who
has sent a short, detailed synopsis. I can read five synopses in the time it takes me
to read a full script, so I'll always put off the full script until I can find the time to
read it—sometimes as much as months later when I can devote a full day to reading
scripts. If I like the synopsis then I'll contact the writer and ask to see a full script.

Each individual must decide just what he or she wishes to include and what message
about him or herself to convey in the cover letter. Remember that your creativity as a
writer can serve you well in your cover letter. It is your first opportunity to "hook" the
reader. But keep in mind that the cover letter is also business correspondence, so don't
go overboard creatively.

Here are some points to remember when constructing your cover letter:

• Keep your letter brief, typed, well-written, and follow business letter format.
Grammatical and spelling errors do little to interest an editor. Proofread your cover
letter carefully.

• Include your contact information—full name, address, and phone number. This can be

Be sure that when you submit a proposal that it's done in a professional manner—typed, double-spaced, easy to read, and professional looking.

Another thing I like to see from potential writers is a "comics" resume. If a writer has been published, then I'd like to know about it.

Also, since I generally work with smaller publishers, those who tend to give new talent a chance, I generally don't pair writers and artists together. A lot of the small publishers are like this. If you want to submit something to me or other small publishers, then it's a good idea to already be working with an artist and submit both your story and his/her art at the same time. So ideally, what I would like to see is a detailed, short synopsis of your story with a few pages of art samples from the artist of your choice and, if possible, a listing of comics credits for both the writer and the artist.

Kilroy Is Here *art by Andrew Robinson*

in the form of letterhead or added as a part of the body of the letter.

- Introduce yourself (e.g., "I am a 20-year-old college student. . .").

- Provide a brief description of your education and related work experience.

- Describe your specific work interests and willingness to continually work at improving your skills.

- Briefly outline the enclosed proposal and sample contents. Here's your chance to really hook the editor. Make sure your title piques the editor's interest to look for more.

- Conclude with a courteous salutation.

Scott Peterson, Editor, Batman Group Liaison for DC Comics
Credits Include: *Detective Comics, Batman Adventures, Green Arrow, The Huntress, Batman v. Predator II* for DC Comics.

Question: Do you think it is beneficial for a writer to team up with an artist when submitting work? Should the artist be an established pro, or are newcomers preferred?

A new writer should do absolutely anything he or she can to break into this industry. It is so much harder for a writer than an artist to break in, that anything a writer can do to get someone to look at his or her work is a good thing. Obviously it's preferable to team up with an experienced artist, but even if the artist is a newcomer, it will help to get someone to take a quick look at your writing.

On the flip side, a new artist probably shouldn't hook up with a new writer, since an editor tends to want an artist to be available for anything. The artist might feel loyalty toward the writer, but the editor just might not think that the writer is ready. If it's an experienced writer, then the artist should absolutely hook up with them. For example, we will look very seriously at any artist that Alan Grant recommends. He's been in the business long enough so that if he says an artist is pretty good, we know he's going to be good. And obviously we want to keep Alan happy. But when it's a new-writer/new-artist team, more often than not, it's the artist who is going to get the attention.

However, even though it's better for a writer to team up with a known artist, teaming up with a new artist is still better than coming in cold, completely on his/her own. But if the writer can hook up with someone like Kevin Nolan, that's the best thing in the world.

Art from Batman *promotional poster*

- Remember, the more time they spend reading your cover letter, the less time they'll spend reading your samples.

Read outside of comics. The only way to do good work is to read widely. If all you read is comics or all you read is books you're not going to make it, if you want to be a comic writer. You've got to have some sense of something bigger than your own field or area. I think that's what makes people original and different and therefore good: they bring different things to their writing.

JOE R. LANSDALE,
Writer

The Proposal or Outline

The proposal or outline is probably the most crucial portion of your sample. If the editor has decided to look at your sample, this is your one big opportunity to show your stuff. Sometimes editors will bypass the cover letter and go straight to this part of an unsolicited submission, only returning to the cover letter if they have been impressed by the work in the proposal.

Your proposal or outline should be a single page, double-spaced. It should describe the story or series (i.e., whether it is eight pages or a single comic issue) that you want to write. The content should be geared specifically to the type of material the target company publishes. Be sure that your genre and style fits with the company's guidelines (from which you should be working)! For a detailed example of a proposal/outline, see Chapter Two.

Scripting Samples

The final portion of your sample should be an example of your scripting abilities. This section is very important since you will not be including a full script of your proposed work. The one or two pages of sample script demonstrate to the editor that you have the knowledge and skills necessary to develop your proposal into script form. It also shows that you are familiar with scripting styles accepted by the comics industry.

Hone your craft and learn the rigors and language of writing for comics. And be a professional: know what your limitations are and deliver on deadline. Nothing will sink you faster—even if you're very, very talented—than not being able to deliver your work on time.

JERRY PROSSER
Writer

It is advised that you familiarize yourself with the scripting style preferred by a particular target company. Ask around with established professionals, at conventions or store appearances, to find out whether a publisher prefers full-style over plot-style scripts. Try to tailor your samples to the preferences of that particular company when submitting your samples.

It is a valuable skill to be able to script in both styles. Additionally, some professionals like to develop a style that is characteristically their own—sometimes incorporating attributes of both scripting formats. However when in doubt, utilize the full-style script method. It's always better to give them more than less when demonstrating your scripting knowledge. (See Chapter Two for examples of full-style and plot-style scripting.)

There is nothing more distracting to an editor than getting a proposal or writing submission, that is full of spelling, grammar, and punctuation errors. I would advise aspiring writers to fix up their grammar, and become educated about the language with which they are working. Language is a tool for a writer, and a writer who doesn't know grammar or spelling is basically working with a deficient tool. If I have two neophyte writers to choose from, and the quality of their stories is about the same, I'm going to go with the one who understands grammar, spelling, and punctuation.

DIANA SCHUTZ
Editor-in-Chief for Dark Horse Comics

METHODS OF PRESENTATION

With the exception of the cover letter, which should always follow established business correspondence format, your samples can take a variety of presentation forms. The choice is a personal one, but should be guided by the idea that the more professional and businesslike your submission, the more likely you will be considered seriously. Remember that it's not the gimmicks or the eye-catching design that will ultimately sell the editor, but your demonstrated ability to write a solid story, with a clear conflict and resolution defined by an identifiable beginning, middle, and end. Your skill as a writer is your greatest asset—not your access to office supplies and computer design software!

It is recommended that your sample presentation follow a simple format. Your cover letter page should be loose, while your proposal/outline and scripting pages should be stapled together. Stay away from colored papers and graphic design elements. Make sure that your spacing and margins are sufficient to keep the appearance of the page open, not claustrophobic. It's sometimes tempting to reduce margins or line spacing to fit more information onto a page, but resist that urge. Demonstrate your skills as a writer by further refining your sample to fit the allowed space, rather than tailoring the space to fit your sample. Make sure that each and every page of your sample bears your name and contact information. It is also helpful to include a page number. You may also want to include a total page count (i.e., page 3 of 4) to help the editor keep track of the sample pages should they become separated.

The presentation of the sample is also dictated by whether you are handing out or mailing your sample. If you are handing out your samples in person, at a convention, for example, it is not necessary to include a cover letter because you act as the "cover letter," and your ability to interest the person influences your chances of having your work considered.

TYPES OF COMICS PUBLISHED

There are a wide variety of comic types being published in our industry today. Additionally, each publisher has its own names for the various formats, which can cause some confusion (e.g., Prestige Format vs. Premium Format vs. Deluxe Format). Here is a checklist with a brief description of a number of the more popular forms.

Ongoing Series: Regular series featuring a regular character(s) in a variety of story situations. May feature related spin-off titles.

Limited Series or Mini-Series: A special, short series that features a regular character(s) in a special story line, and often with unusual art. Usually features two or more issues.

One-Shot: Same as a Limited Series, but a self-contained single issue. Sometimes features a longer page count.

Graphic Novel: Same as a Limited Series, but usually a single, large issue. Size is usually 48 or more pages.

Anthology: A single comic issue that can be of varying page lengths—but is usually the standard 24 pages—and features more than one story. Often features more than one specific character as well.

Collected Volume: A single, bound collection of the books from an Ongoing or Limited Series. Often features original art for the cover.

BUSINESS CARDS AND LOGOS

Although many aspiring writers may feel that artistic business cards are the venue of the aspiring artist, they should think again. First, a business card is probably one of the most critical tools a professional can employ. A business card provides your contact information to potential employers, new industry contacts, peers, and businesses. Business cards are fairly inexpensive to produce, especially for simple black and whites, and you can usually get a price break if you order larger amounts.

Think of your business card as a little billboard. Take the opportunity to maximize that display space with what distinguishes you—your writing skills. It doesn't hurt to have an interesting logo or art design either. Anything that will draw attention to the card and encourage people to read the information printed there—your name and occupation. Keep in mind, people like to look at business card art. So make your card unique and increase the chances that the recipient will remember you. (See examples of business cards for writers on page 64.)

John Ostrander, Freelance Writer

Credits Include: *Suicide Squad* (with Kim Yale), *Wasteland*, *Firestorm*,
The Spectre, Gotham Nights II from DC Comics; *Magnus Robot Fighter*,
Rai, Eternal Warrior from Valiant; *Elf Quest: Jink* from Warp
Graphics; *Grimjack* from First Comics; *Bishop* mini-series, *Wolverine*
graphic novel (with Tom Mandrake) from Marvel Comics.

Question: Do you use a business card or sample pack when
approaching potential publishers? Do you think they make a difference
in acquiring work?

I don't use this tactic, but at this point I've been in the business so long that
people know who I am. Once folks get to know your work, it's more likely
that they'll at least listen to your ideas, and at that point a sample pack is no
longer necessary. I think it would be helpful for newcomers, though.
Particularly if it's well-organized and professionally presented and if it's a copy
the recipient is not required to return.

However, I do have a business card that I find very useful. This way
whoever I'm talking to, particularly people with whom I want to work—an
artist or another writer, or somebody you meet at a convention—I have some
way to pass along my contact information. You can easily have them made in a
business card vending machine—the sort of thing where you can get about 50
cards for about five dollars. So there's no excuse not to at least have a business
card. It does give you a more professional air and it gives editors something
they can put in their Rolodex, something concrete that they can file away.

Art by Tom Mandrake from Spectre #0, *DC Comics*

**Tom Mason, Writer and Co-founder of MainBrain Productions.
Formerly Creative Director for Malibu Comics Entertainment, Inc. a
division of Marvel Entertainment.**
Credits Include: *Dinosaurs for Hire* (creator), *Prototype* (co-creator)
for Malibu Comics.

Question: Do you look for a business card and/or sample pack from
new writers who approach you for work? Does it make a difference
what type of approach they use?

Tom Mason

When I'm talking to writers who are actively looking for
work, I need to see both a business card and sample material,
preferably published. It does make a difference as to what
kind of approach a writer should use. For a new writer
making a "cold" approach to an editor, especially at a
convention, it's best to keep things simple and brief: a quick
introduction, delivery of the samples, a brief conversation,
and then move on to make your next contact.

Conventions cause sensory overload and there are so many
things to do that it's easy to be distracted. The last thing
anybody wants to hear is a new writer going on and on about the minute
details of the proposal he's just handed in.

*Something that has profoundly influenced me and which I've tried to integrate
into my own work, is what Jack Kirby once advised me: "Do it your own way.
Remember, the companies need you. They need your creativity. Only you know
the way your ideas should be expressed, so maintain your independence."*

*Companies will try to homogenize your work, and it's important that you
stay true to your vision. This is as much a business decision as a creative
decision, because ownership of your characters and controlling your concepts
will eventually lead to a better exploitation of your characters.*

LEN STRAZEWSKI
Writer

Business cards are indispensable. Keep a few in your pockets and wallet or bag.
Always keep them handy. Remember that they provide you with an easy way to give
your contact information to a prospective employer. When you meet a prospective
employer, or another professional, you speak volumes about your level of
professionalism and business acumen if you can say "Oh, here's my card." Always hand
a card to any prospect that looks at your samples, and always include one when you
hand out your samples.

An acquaintance of mine, an aspiring prose writer, finally took my advice and had some really nice cards made up before attending a large convention. He was stunned by the response and said he could kick himself for having waited so long. He made some excellent work connections—and even got a few lunch invites from editors!

At conventions I have attended, I've been delighted by some of the very creative business cards I've seen. Some writers have utilized clip art libraries to find a business card logo (using art featuring typewriters, pens, pencils, quills, inkpots, paper scrolls, and computers). Some have hired professional artists or had an aspiring artist friend design a logo for their cards. Some writers have made use of specialty design papers and cards, in conjunction with a laser printer, to produce smaller batches of business cards. Some business cards have even been simply labeled with a statement of skills (e.g., Writer, Poet, Scripts, etc.).

Examples of creative business card designs

Whichever route you decide to take, just be sure to have a business card. It tells the recipient, "I am a business professional."

Don't ever get discouraged, and don't expect tons of money. You should really love comics. With few exceptions, this is not a business that makes folks a lot of money. If you're in comics expecting to make heaps of money, then you're in the wrong industry. But if you love it, stay with it and you'll make it.

ROLAND MANN
Writer/Editor, Malibu Comics

Tearsheets

For those of you who may be unfamiliar with the term, a tearsheet is simply a published copy of your work. There are some aspiring professionals who have managed to get some of their work published. It may not be much; a small company might have published it—even one now out of business—or it may even be a self-published effort, but published work is an excellent inclusion for your samples if it is good. If it's a far cry from your usual caliber of work, mention the credit in your cover letter, but don't include the work unless the prospective employer specifically asks to see it. If the publisher did a hatchet job editing the work, you may want to include a sample page of the unedited script so that a comparison can be made.

Published samples are very useful. They indicate to a potential employer that you've made the effort to get work in the past and completed the assignment to that publisher's satisfaction. Granted the experience may not have been a positive one—with problems getting paid by the publisher, meeting your deadline, or even getting your complimentary copies—but it helps to provide the appearance of professionalism on your part. Make the best of a bad experience and make it work to your benefit in the future.

Persistence. Any writer trying to break into the business has to realize that he or she will be rejected a lot before landing a job. Expect that and be prepared to deal with it. If the writer is really committed to breaking in, then he/she should just keep hammering away at it.

JOHN MOORE
Writer

Sample Packets

Sample packets are a useful way to handle your personal sample submissions. A sample packet is composed of your proposal/outline, examples of your scripting, and your business card. You may also want to include copies of tearsheets if you have any. These packets should be stapled together. Carry a supply of these with you when approaching professionals in person—at conventions, store appearances or personal interviews. It is a sign of good business skills to be prepared. Having your sample packet on hand makes contact with a professional effortless for both you and the recipient. And by preparing these packets ahead of time, you are assured of never being caught unaware.

Denis Kitchen, Publisher, Kitchen Sink Press, Inc.
Credits Include: Kitchen Sink Press highlights include Will Eisner's
graphic novel series *A Contract with God, A Life Force,* and *To the
Heart of the Storm; Xenozoic Tales* (a.k.a. *Cadillacs & Dinosaurs*) by
Mark Schultz; *From Hell* by Alan Moore and Eddie Campbell; *Blood
Club* and *Black Hole* by Charles Burns; collections of classic comics
and strips by Harvey Kurtzman, Alex Raymond, Milton Caniff, Al
Capp, and others; *Understanding Comics* by Scott McCloud; *The Crow*
by James O'Barr.

Question: Do you think it is beneficial for a writer to team up with an
artist when submitting work? Should the artist be an established pro,
or are newcomers preferred?

Frankly, I prefer an *auteur* who can both write and draw, such as a Will Eisner
or a Mark Schultz. My own career began as a writer/artist and virtually all of the
"underground" cartoonists during my company's early history wrote their own
material. Nevertheless, I acknowledge that two heads can often be as good as
one. If a writer does not have a preexisting working relationship with an artist
and we are impressed with his or her written proposal, we will endeavor to find
an artist appropriate for the project. In such instances, a comics publisher's role
can be that of a matchmaker.

One example is our pairing of playwright James Vance and artist Dan Burr on
Kings in Disguise. We loved Vance's proposal and looked for an artist who we
felt had the right drawing style for Vance's depression-era material. But style
alone was insufficient. We knew that this particular project would take a year or
more to complete and needed a personality to fit as well. Our instincts were right
and the Vance/Burr collaboration not only led to an award-winning series and
collection, but a personal friendship between the collaborators. This kind of
matchmaking, done right, can be time-consuming (i.e., costly). But when the
results are wonderful, a publisher can take a special pride in both supporting and
shaping the creative process.

If a writer and artist have mutual respect for each other's abilities they are far
more inclined to do superior work than teams arbitrarily slapped together in an
assembly line, supervised by an uninspired editor or publisher. So I encourage
self-generated teams to stick together as long as it works or they have mutual
confidence in their prospects.

I have no strong preference about whether a writer works with a newcomer versus an established pro. The former can be fresh and innovative, or alarmingly amateurish. The latter can be solidly professional, or tired and hackneyed. An artist's experience alone is not a key to collaborative success if the writer does not trust his or her own eye. The experienced pro will be much more likely to demand payment in advance or upon completion of their work, whereas a newcomer is more likely to work on a speculative basis. Since the question presumes the work has not yet been accepted and contracted by a publisher, then this means the economic burden will be on the writer who must hire, or form a formal partnership with, the artist.

The primary downside of a joint writer/artist proposal for a writer is that it will almost certainly be judged as a whole and may be rejected on the basis of the art alone. If the pair receive a worthless form rejection letter, or deal with a less-than-candid editor, the writer may never know that his or her ideas were ruined by ineffective visuals. Of course the opposite can also happen, when great art is dragged down by a deficient script.

The upside of submitting an already illustrated script is that such a proposal automatically has a better chance of being examined quickly and selected for publication, either because it is simply a successful collaboration or because it is cheaper for a publisher and easier for a lazy editor.

Art from Mark Schultz' Xenozoic Tales published by Kitchen Sink Press

APPROACHING POTENTIAL EMPLOYERS

There are a variety of paths that you, as an aspiring comics writer, can take to acquire work in the industry. Although each route has its pros and cons, there are some that are more likely to produce work. However, as an earnest freelancer, you should be pursuing as many of these avenues as possible. The more angles you take, the more you increase your exposure in the industry. Let's take a closer look at the four main methods of approaching potential employers in the comics industry: conventions, mail route, personal interviews and working for a publisher.

CONVENTIONS

Although each of the three main methods of approaching potential employers has its strengths, "working" a convention is probably the most valuable for a writer who wishes to work as a freelancer. Despite the misconception that artists have better chances at conventions than writers, because of the visual nature of their work, the convention is equally valuable to a writer. The social/personal aspects of a convention are where that value lies.

Get out there and meet editors. Establish yourself as a person, with an identity, so that they will remember you, and you won't just be some anonymous sample sitting on their desk.

JOHN MOORE
Writer

There are a variety of ways to search for work at a convention. These include introducing yourself to publishers and editors, using the proper business etiquette to show your work, and using professional feedback to improve your chances. To get started, however, it is imperative that you understand the importance of attending conventions and how they can benefit your burgeoning career. Since conventions represent the most powerful way to pursue work, they merit a detailed examination.

Roland Mann, Writer and Publisher of Silverline Comics
Credits Include: *Miss Fury*, Genesis line *(Protectors, Ferret, Ex-Mutants)* Ultraverse line *(Sludge, Nightman)*, *Battletech* for Malibu Comics; *Cat and Mouse* for EF Graphics and Malibu Comics; *Switchblade* for Silverline Comics.

Question: How important a role do you feel conventions play for an aspiring writer, and what advice would you give on attending?

Conventions are very important. Especially for writers. I think that part of the skill of breaking in is actually shaking hands with and getting to know the people [in the industry]. It's tougher for a writer. An artist has something very visual to show. A writer can't just say, "Have you got two minutes to take a look at this?" People can't tell how good the writing is just by taking a quick look at the words on the page, because they have to spend some time reading. At conventions, a writer can get out there and meet the people. Be nice—basically, be a salesman—so professionals will take time out to really look at your work. You have to go to conventions, meet editors and other professionals. And you shouldn't go with the intention of meeting editors exclusively. Granted, editors can give you the assignments. However, other freelancers, other creators, can put in a great word for you. Or you might meet someone who decides they'd like to do a project with you. As a writer, if you can get an artist to team up with, it's generally a lot easier to sell to any interested party. For all these reasons, conventions are a must.

Your strategy for attending should start with a list of your own preferences. First decide which conventions you want to attend. Conventions start advertising early in the year, so you should be subscribing to publications like the *Comics Buyer's Guide*. They run lists of upcoming conventions and who's going to be in attendance. Choose the folks that you want to meet, that you've heard good things about; folks with whom you want to spend a couple of minutes talking. Target those conventions for attending. It might be tough, financially. Chances are you're going to have to say, "Hey best buddy, let's share a room at this convention." If the only way you can afford to go to a convention is to crash with two or three people in one room, then that's a necessary sacrifice, because you must go to conventions. You have to meet the industry people and shake their hands.

Put together a list of the top five conventions this year that you want to attend. Then start making plans to go to the first one. Take them one at a time. If you know you're going to be attending these conventions all year long, take advantage of the occasional airfare wars. Keep a close eye on that, and you can get a pretty inexpensive round-trip ticket. I know that I wasn't able to afford full airfare when I started out. The way I was able to go to the first Chicago Con was with a friend of mine, Steven Butler. He was given a comp room from First Comics, for whom he was working at the time. He graciously allowed me to crash in the room with him. My only cost then was my plane ticket. I was able to get one on sale. If that hadn't been available to me, then I probably would have never gone to that convention.

Organize your list of conventions in a prioritized order, and then find any way you can to get to those conventions. You'll find that there are a lot of really cool people in the industry. Sure, there are some jerks, but generally there are just a lot of really good folks who are interested in seeing others succeed. A lot of people in comics have a mentor-type attitude, which is really great for newcomers. This is a creative field, and everyone has their opinions. I think you should listen to it all, and then develop your own perspective from what you learn. This process can only happen at a convention.

Once at the convention, you should aggressively hand out business cards and short samples. Don't ever give anyone a 50-page script of their character; just because you think your work is great and that they'll have time to read it, doesn't mean that it is acceptable. Nobody's going to have time to read 50 pages. The shorter your sample, the better off you will be at getting someone, anyone, to read the material. If you have three nutshell plots on one page, you're more likely to have somebody read your work than if they are five pages long. Chances are that 15 pages are going to get put in a stack of work to be read. The person [who takes the sample] will probably be very friendly to you, and insist they'll read it, but they're not going to be able to do it. If you have a much shorter sample, your chances are much better of getting the material read.

What Is a Convention?

In our industry, we are fortunate to have an extensive convention circuit. The convention circuit is the variety of events, featuring comic content, held throughout the year, around the country and the world. A local sponsor organizes the event, which includes a show of comics (and comic-related material), comic sellers, publishers, and the creators. These shows are open to the public and frequented by fans of the genre, collectors, and curiosity-seekers. The sponsor can charge a range of entrance fees for attending these events contingent on a variety of factors, including size, duration, numbers of retailers and professionals attending, and the level of "stardom" of the guest professionals.

Conventions are held everywhere and range dramatically in size. However, for purposes of simplicity I will concentrate on information specific to the United States.

Also, continue to approach the same people you may have met at other conventions. Just because you talked with them previously doesn't matter. Go ahead and give them another [sample] package. After the third time or so, they're going to begin to remember your name. And name recognition is important for getting work in comics.

Follow that up with mail samples every four to six weeks. Even if you don't get a reply, don't worry about it. It all applies toward the goal of name recognition. If you continue to put your name in front of someone they're going to be saying, "Oh, yeah. I know this guy. He keeps sending me stuff." Eventually, they'll say, "Well, let me take a look at it this time." So following up after a convention is real helpful, since it reinforces that name recognition. And chances are that whomever you handed your samples to at a show doesn't have it anymore—they probably did not make it back to the office. Conventions are busy for everybody, and your samples aren't the number one thing on an editor's mind when they're traveling between the office and a convention. So wait a couple of weeks, and then send a package through the mail.

Cover from Switchblade *#2*

Your town or city may be the site of many different conventions throughout the year, or they may be held only occasionally. In the U.S., there are a variety of well-known conventions held each year. Some of the larger, more established conventions include The Big Apple Comic Convention held in New York twice a year; HeroesCon held in Charlotte, North Carolina, each summer; Mid Ohio Con in Columbus, Ohio, each fall and WonderCon held in Oakland, California, every spring. Wizard World (held in Chicago every July) and the San Diego Comic-Con (which usually runs in August) are the two largest shows in the U.S. In addition, there are shows in many other major cities, including Atlanta and Bethesda, Maryland. Major conventions represent most geographic areas of the country.

THE ANATOMY OF A CONVENTION

Most conventions are structured in a similar way, despite different special events that may be scheduled. There are usually four main components to any convention: the dealer/retailers room, the publisher's area, the guest area/artists alley, and panels and displays.

1. The Retailers

There is usually an area designated for retailers (the guys who sell the goods). These are important people. They represent the customers who will ultimately buy your product. It is vital to keep in mind that they are a crucial component in your employment. They ultimately decide which product to order from the distributors and publishers. Cultivating a positive and friendly relationship with retailers ensures that your latest project will be remembered when ordering time rolls around.

2. The Publishers

Depending on the size of the function, there may be representatives from a few or most of the comics publishers in our industry. The publishers set up display areas to promote their latest properties and provide sneak previews of upcoming projects. They also structure their convention time to consider work from newcomers, and often will be on the lookout for new talent while attending a show.

In the case of our largest convention, the San Diego Comic-Con, it is unusual for a publisher to be absent. Therefore, the larger shows, despite their greater cost to attend, are often the best places to seek employment.

3. The Creators

Most shows use "name" artists and writers as a drawing card for the public. Sometimes they bring in guests who are the latest hot talent, and sometimes the guest is a popular favorite who has been around for years. Depending on the size of the function, there can be one or two main guests or, in the case of the much larger shows like those held in Chicago and San Diego, there may be a whole flotilla of big names present. Some will be guests of the show, and some will simply be appearing as part of their own self-promotion and to maintain contact with their readers.

Creators can offer some very valuable insights into the business. Long-established pros have a wealth of useful information and valuable advice. Their input can be very helpful to a newcomer.

As a writer, it is important to remember that insights can be had from both writers and artists. An artist may not be able to offer you specific writing advice, but they can make business suggestions that can help increase your chances of being considered for work.

4. Panel Discussions and Displays

Many conventions offer a variety of programming events. Some conventions combine sports memorabilia, science fiction/horror, gaming, or media (i.e., movies, TV, video, genre magazines) as part of their panel and display presentations. Whatever the content, many cons offer programming in the form of panel discussions. Panels generally feature authorities (and I use this term loosely!) on the topic of discussion, who present information, discuss it among themselves, and answer questions from the audience.

ARTISTS: SOME SPECIAL ADVICE FOR A WRITER GETTING STARTED

It is almost a unanimous opinion in the editorial end of comics that having an artist illustrate a novice writer's script can significantly improve their chances of being considered, when the samples are an unsolicited submission.

The reason is quite simple. Comics publishing is a business where the over-worked editorial staff have very little free time for considering unsolicited material. When they do manage to find a snippet of free time, they will most likely try to work their way quickly through their growing slush pile. An artist's rendition of your script will improve your chances of being noticed. Sad as it is to say, it's a fact of comic industry life: A quick glance at your story laid out in pictures is more likely to hook the editor than any masterful combination of words. Human beings are a very vision-dependent species. As a result, images that can be processed instantly will have a much greater (and more immediate) impression upon us. And so it is with editors.

If you do decide to have an artist illustrate your work, editors advise that your chances will be improved even more if that artist is a proven, established professional. If you manage to convince (or hire) a name professional to illustrate your script, and include a copy of that page of comic art, you will be more likely to quickly interest an editor—particularly if they happen to be familiar with that artist.

If you only have access to an unproven newcomer, even that can be beneficial. Just remember to use an artist whose work you feel is of sufficient quality to garner interest. But keep in mind the flip side of this coin: The artist may acquire work immediately while you, the writer, may not. If you and the artist enter this sample-generating agreement with a full understanding of the possible outcomes, you will have no problems. Additionally, if the artist is a friend who acquires work through your association, he will then represent a potential industry contact for you. Cultivate relationships with your peers, and work together to promote each other. At some point, in the not-so-distant future, you may find that your early collaborations have served you both well in your respective careers!

Panel members can include publishers, editors, creators, and knowledgeable fans.

Panels are valuable tools for the newcomer. Since topics range anywhere from simple entertainment to discussions of the business of the comics industry, they can be a precious source of information and insight. They can also provide an open forum for questioning individuals who might not otherwise be accessible to you. Learn to listen carefully; much useful information is available at a panel discussion.

Displays at conventions can mean a variety of things. They can take the form of an art gallery displaying originals from attending and non-attending professionals. It can mean an exhibit of memorabilia. It can also mean a demonstration by a creator. You are about to embark on a career in a visual industry. Just because your area of expertise will be words, you should not ignore the visual aspects of this business.

Check out what is offered by the convention programming and don't spend your whole time dogging the heels of a potential employer. There's a lot to be learned on the road to becoming a professional, and the more useful information you can find, the better you'll be at your job.

No matter the size, frequency, or structure of conventions in your area, one thing is abundantly clear: Attending a convention is one of the most important methods of securing work in the comic industry.

Learn and implement self-promotion and self-marketing techniques as much as possible. Even though the writer is essentially the first rung of the ladder in comics, they are easily the first person to be overshadowed in so many ways. It can be so hard to present yourself, even once you're established. You've got to be very savvy, in terms of creating an impression of what you've done, and what you continue to do. Otherwise, I think you can easily fall into a void just as easily as you got your break. Or just as bad, you can end up in a holding pattern for years where you're just doing the same thing as when you started. That's fine for a lot of people, but from an artistic point of view it's damning. It can be very damaging to your self-esteem, and you don't grow as a writer.

But if you take some time to create a press file, a portfolio of what you've done before—even if you don't have a track record yet—you can change your job outlook. Maybe you've won some writing contests, or gotten some notices in a local paper. Even though you don't want to go up to an editor and wave the Poughkeepsie Journal *in his face, you can present that information as ". . . has received awards in local writing symposiums." Use language to your advantage.*

I think that self-promotion can be tremendously useful, and applicable outside of comics. I think comics are a terrific medium, but they aren't the only outlets for writers. With other opportunities opening up, you can use your promotional material to leapfrog back and forth. You can even use that first comics job to get work in other fields, like gaming or info-tainment software for example, while you're still building your comic career. You can always use that to your advantage, but that's not going to happen if you don't have the skills to market yourself and what you've done.

D.G. Chichester
Writer/Editor

Many established professionals will tell you just how critical attending industry shows can be. A friend of mine—a relative newcomer to the field of comics writing—finally broke down and agreed to attend a variety of conventions including Wizard World in Chicago, the Atlanta DragonCon, and the San Diego Comic-Con. Although he did not line up a major job at these events, the personal connections he made have proved invaluable to him, and he has acquired a variety of comics writing jobs as a result.

For many aspiring professionals, it's also not feasible to make the trip to a publisher, let alone trying to secure an appointment time for an interview. Because of the way editors structure their time at conventions, this is an ideal opportunity to distribute your samples. It can save you the expense of an unannounced (and likely wasted) trip to the publisher's city, or the aggravation of being on a "waiting list" for an interview. Plus, it provides the opportunity to approach more than one publisher at a time.

Besides showing your work, a convention provides another critical element to getting work in the industry: networking. Networking is the opportunity to socialize, make contacts, introduce yourself, and, finally, familiarize yourself with the way things are done in the industry. The more knowledgeable you are as a newcomer, the more respect you'll gain, and the more likely you'll be considered for work over other newcomers.

ProFile

Clydene Nee, Colorist and Graphic Designer
Credits Include: *Ultraman*, *SeaQuest* for Harvey Comics; *Images of Shadowhawk* for Image's Shadowline; *Image Universe Cards* for Topps; *Hellshock #2* and *Image #0* for Image; *Melonpool Chronicles* (publisher). In Color clients included: Dark Horse Comics, Image, Comico, Now Comics, Hero, Malibu Comics, Harvey Comics. Clydene has also worked for Wildstorm Productions and Top Cow creating posters, ads, postcards, and trading cards.

Question: How important a role do you feel conventions play for an aspiring comics writer, and what advice would you give about attending?

I think they're very important. It's true that conventions are where you may be able to get an editor to look at your stuff, but more importantly you have a chance to have your peers look at your work. I had never shown my work at the San Diego Con. Then one year I went to WonderCon and sat next to Charles Vess, and he got a chance to see my work. It was really, really beneficial for me to get his input. I think that if you're a writer, you need to be willing to show your work to your peers.

Of course, there is also the importance of meeting editors. Just keep in mind that you can't be too pushy. There are a lot of editors at shows, and they're generally really busy—even schmoozing with their own artists and writers. They can be really put off by how many newcomers can be "glad-hands" at a convention. You have to make sure they know who you are of course, but without being obnoxious or hanging around all the time. And you certainly shouldn't follow them everywhere, because that can be kind of frightening. And whatever you do, don't follow them into the bathroom! A very high-profile comic professional told me once that he can't really go to the bathroom at conventions anymore, because fans and folks looking for work will just follow him in there and bother him. Just remember to keep the setting appropriate.

Attending the Convention

The first consideration before you attend a convention is to ensure that your writing samples are prepared and that you are well stocked with sample packs and business cards. Then, before you head out, prepare a strategy.

Consider the length of the show, which potential employers you would like to approach for work consideration, which professionals you'd like to meet and talk with, and any programming events you are interested in attending. Do not plan to spend the whole time chasing down one elusive lead. Set aside time—keeping in mind the schedules of the publishers and editors—to pursue prospective work, and then use the rest of the time for looking, listening, and networking (also called "schmoozing" in more casual circles).

A good strategy is to take a little extra time to look through the program book, if possible, before the convention begins. This will help you organize your time more effectively. Once the doors are opened, try to avoid the big rush to the most popular locations. The crowds will thin out a bit as time passes, and you can have a more leisurely conversation with your target employer or pro. Then, consider following these steps:

1. Introducing Yourself and Handing Out Your Sample Packs

Your first step should be to stop by each publisher and introduce yourself. Explain your interest, and ask to leave a sample pack with them. Most publishers will be happy to accept your packet, although some may decline and insist on receiving it via the mail. Some publishers will direct you to the New Submissions Editor. Some will state that the company is not accepting new written material. Regardless of the response, be polite, thank them for their time, and ask them if you can leave your business card. Your politeness and businesslike demeanor will make an impression. Even though you may not secure work with that company at that moment, you have taken the first step in laying groundwork for a social relationship—and that will be of value to you as your time in the industry proceeds.

If the publisher seems receptive, and you have a brief written sample, ask if they can take a quick look and give you feedback on your work. This will be even more effective if you have an artist's rendition of your work. The ability to quickly glance at a visual interpretation of your writing can be a very powerful hook, and you may find that it is of great help in keeping a potential publisher's interest during a busy convention.

If the publisher appears interested, but seems swamped with interruptions and distractions, ask for a specific time to return and discuss your work when you will be able to talk uninterrupted. If they are receptive, suggest lunch, coffee, or just a five-minute break away from the melee at their booth or table. If the publisher is agreeable, you're in luck. But try not to take advantage of your good fortune—or misconstrue its meaning. Be businesslike and attentive. The publisher will be pleased that their opinion matters to you, that you were businesslike and friendly, and will remember your meeting for future contacts.

2. Professional Critiques

Take time to approach pros appearing at the show for feedback on your work. They aren't interested in hiring you, but they are often willing to provide you with constructive feedback on your samples. Make sure you wait for a moment when they aren't inundated with people—signing, doing artwork, conversing with attendees—before you approach them for a critique. If the pro is distracted, they won't be able to give your work the full attention it deserves. Choose your timing carefully to make the best use of their time.

Make sure that the samples you present for a critique are brief. Most professionals will be intimidated by a hefty tome slapped on the table, and will postpone or excuse themselves from any critique. If your samples are brief your chances of a critique from a creator improve significantly.

Choose your editors with extreme care. A great editor can make almost any project worthwhile. A bad editor can make your life a torturous hell.

KELLEY PUCKETT
Writer

Keep in mind that just because your samples are in the form of written work doesn't mean that artists won't be helpful in critiquing your work. Many artists can offer you business advice for approaching potential employers that applies to all creators. Additionally, most artists have experience working with comics writers, have developed friendships with those writers, and as a result have valuable insights they can pass along about the pitfalls and pathways those writers may have experienced. Finally, many artists in the comic industry are also writers, or are aspiring writers. For these reasons, they can offer advice and critiques that can be very helpful. Most important though, is the social connection that comes from having a creator look at your work. They may see something that impresses them, and that type of connection can result in promotion of you and your work with their publisher(s).

Remembering that critiques of your work by established professionals can be very valuable, try not to be anxious. Most pros will be honest, since they are comfortably secure in their work, and won't feel threatened by a potential newcomer. If your work has strengths, you'll hear about them. You'll hear about the weaknesses, too. If you present your work to an established pro for critique, be prepared for just that. Although they aren't interested in hiring you, they do remember what it was like getting started. Most pros are eager to help any newcomer who is prepared to work at both the business and their craft. But help takes on a variety of forms, and here it will be (hopefully) a constructive review of your samples.

Listen carefully to their critique, you can even make notes if it'll help you remember, and absorb any useful information on improving your skills. Keep in mind that they are established pros, which means that they've used the skills they're trying to impart to you to gain employment in this industry. This alone should be some indicator of the validity of their comments. On the other hand, keep in mind that people can make mistakes. If a suggestion or comment seems too far off base, or confuses you, consider getting a second opinion. After the convention is over, review everything you've learned from both the creators and publishers. Disregard anything you deem not useful, and extract the information that will best help you to pursue work in the industry.

3. Panels and Displays

Frequently, panels are made up of publishers and creators in the comic industry. The number of panel topics is seemingly infinite. Review your program information, and choose those panels with subjects you think might be useful, or which feature professionals from whom you hope to gain insight. Try to attend the panel with some questions planned that are related to the topic. During the panel listen carefully, and pay attention to any information that can help you in your quest for employment. Feel free to ask questions, but keep in mind that there is an established topic, and that this is a public forum. Other members of the audience are unlikely to be interested in your unrelated personal inquiries.

Also, take time to attend any pertinent displays set up at the convention. If there is an art show, make a point of going. This will give you an opportunity to note the style and genre of work that is being published. Plus, if there are a number of newcomers represented, you may find an artist with which you can team (or whom you can hire) to illustrate your writing samples.

4. Socializing

Although this aspect may be somewhat limited for a nonprofessional, take advantage of any opportunities to mix with publishers and professionals. Frequently, major distributors or retailers, and even publishers, will host functions that enable general attendees to socialize with established pros. If events of this nature are offered, be sure to attend. Make sure you bring a good supply of business cards and a small notepad. But don't bring your writing samples! This is a social event. Make contacts, introduce yourself, hand out business cards, get information, but let the poor pros enjoy some downtime. If you're just itching to show your wares to a particular target, then introduce yourself, explain your interest, and schedule convention time to bring by your samples. But use the social event for just that—socializing.

This is an excellent opportunity for a newcomer, though very few newcomers realize the value of "pressing the flesh." To meet someone on a social level provides you with an opportunity to make an impression outside the convention crowds. You'll become a face with a name, rather than one of the anonymous masses.

Here are some very important points to remember:

* *Prepare a couple of questions and/or comments that you can use as an icebreaker.* If you're short on social skills (i.e., you have trouble carrying your end of a conversation, that sort of thing) then take time before attending an event to familiarize yourself with the professionals and publishers at the convention. That way, if an opportunity to talk presents itself, you have some information you can use to open the conversation. Questions about their interests, current projects, how they work, and past work history

are all good openers. Just remember, most people love to talk about themselves, and a good, interested listener is invaluable. Also, you can make a great contact—even friendship—that could help you down the road professionally.

- *Do not interrupt or hover!* I cannot emphasize enough how annoying this social faux pas can be. If you see a professional you're just dying to talk to, but they're already engrossed in a conversation or otherwise distracted, do not interrupt or hover. If you just have to talk to them, fine. Casually keep an eye on them, and when they are finished, or there is an appropriate moment, then wander over and introduce yourself. Otherwise, wait until the next event or con day. A negative impression of your meeting can carry even more weight in consideration of future work possibilities.

So much of working in comics is luck and timing, because the competition for jobs is so fierce. If you've really got it as a writer (which can mean different things to different editors at different companies) then you should identify the type of genre in which you want to write—even if you want to write in many different genres—then be persistent and approach as many editors and companies as possible.

KAREN BERGER
Executive Editor for DC Comics

- *Don't prolong a "dead" conversation.* If you've managed to start up a conversation, but there is a lull, or apparent disinterest on the part of the pro, then conclude your exchange with the appropriate thanks, and release the poor individual to continue their socializing. Many pros have trouble excusing themselves, and don't want to appear rude. Cut them some slack. Their gratitude will be evident when they look forward to talking with you next time around.

- *Keep it brief.* Although you may be excited and delighted by the chance to have a friendly conversation with an individual who has until now seemed "out of reach," keep in mind that they are at this social event for the same reasons you are. They want to socialize, talk business with editors and publishers, and meet other people. For many professionals living scattered around the country, a convention is often the only opportunity they have to socialize with their peers. So if you get the chance to talk, keep it brief. Be friendly, but don't tie them up for long periods of time. If they seem to be receptive, set a time to meet and let them get back to their "schmoozing" while you continue with yours. I guarantee they'll be grateful, and will remember you in a most positive light when next you meet.

- *Be friendly and businesslike.* If an opportunity to talk with a good contact or a potential employer presents itself, take it in a friendly, but businesslike manner. Introduce yourself (your first and last name), comment on your interest in that individual, and use some of your icebreaker questions and/or comments. When you deem it the appropriate time to depart, offer them your business card, shake hands, and express your pleasure with meeting them and how you look forward to talking again. By following this very simple strategy, you will have left the individual with the impression that you are friendly, businesslike, enthusiastic, and considerate. You will also have primed them for another meeting—hopefully sometime later at the convention. This strategy will provide you with fertile grounds in which to plant the seed of your possible employment.

- *Follow through.* This is absolutely imperative, whether you are socializing, meeting at the convention, or corresponding. Do not expect the individual you contact to follow through for you. The responsibility is yours. You're the one looking for work, and you'll be the one hanging over the phone like a jilted date. Don't sit around waiting anxiously. If you feel you've made a good contact, then follow through while you are still fresh in their mind. If you've talked at an evening social event, then stop by during the next convention day to talk again, briefly. If your contact expresses interest in seeing your work, then visit with them at their earliest convenience during the convention. However you do it, just remember to follow through. Even established pros realize the importance of following through.

FEEDBACK AND CRITIQUES

Responses to your work, both formal (critique) and informal (feedback) are important to the continued improvement of your writing skills. There is absolutely no one who is too good to be critiqued. In order to grow as a writer, and learn to master your craft, you must be willing to take comments from readers—whether they are professionals, friends, or family.

There are a variety of ways to obtain a critique or feedback, including attending conventions and distributing samples of your work, sending in unsolicited mail submissions to potential publishers (although there is not always an immediate response), and in personal interviews. To ensure your growth as a skilled professional, you should seek out feedback from both your peers and potential employers, utilizing any of these venues.

There are three important components to a critique: the anatomy of the actual critique, the expected etiquette, and applying the feedback to improve your work. Here is a brief description of each of these segments.

Anatomy of a Critique
Depending on who does the critique (your Mom or your new boss), the time constraints under which it is done (a crowded convention or a quiet office), and the skill level of the critique-giver (a Pulitzer Prize-winning author or your 10-year-old nephew), the critique is going to vary dramatically in its style. There are many characteristics of a good critique. A good critique will focus on both strengths and weaknesses and look at your improvement over time. It will not be personal and will

Keep in mind that publishers and editors are often doing the work of more than one person. They have little in the way of free time, and no matter how wonderful an impression you've made, it is a courtesy to them to help out in your business relationship by following through. This frees them of the responsibility of trying to remember everyone they've talked to and every little thing they said. They will appreciate your consideration, and by following through you display your professionalism and interest.

THE MAIL ROUTE

Sending samples by mail and introducing yourself via letter, in combination with other methods of approaching possible employers, can also provide a good base for breaking into comics. This gives editors and publishers a chance to peruse your work and mark your progress. But keep in mind, it is very important that you follow the correct procedures and etiquette for mailing samples.

As I mentioned before, conventions are a crucial component in securing work and gaining exposure as a newcomer, and following up on those convention contacts by mail

---

remain objective. A good critique involves looking at a reasonable amount of your work—not too much, not too little—and analyzes not just the mechanics of it but also the overall effect or "big picture." A good critique is a true dialogue, and the critic should be asking for information about you and how you work to better provide constructive advice. Finally, a good critique considers your feelings, without babying you. You should be treated politely, respectfully, and considerately.

Critique Etiquette

As important as it is for a critique to be good, it's equally important for you to follow certain expected etiquette. Remember to temper the unabashed adoration of family and close friends with more objective critiques. Always pay careful attention to the critic. Never interrupt to make excuses or explanations for work that might be criticized. Don't be rude, flippant, or cocky. Self-confidence is fine, but there's a fine line between confidence and arrogance. ABSOLUTELY NEVER compare your work to anyone else's—either positively or negatively. And NEVER, NEVER, criticize the work of the critic. They didn't ask for your input and they're doing you a favor by looking at your work.

Applying Feedback

Take all criticisms with a grain of salt and select the advice that seems to ring most true. Resolve to work on making those recommended changes. The best way of improving your skills is to continually reassess your work. And practice. Practice, practice, practice. Only then will you find your writing skills improving to a level of quality high enough to acquire consistent work in the comics industry.

is very important. This is one place where the mail system is indispensable. If you've been able to attend a convention, and had a chance to meet some publishers and editors with whom you wish to work, now is the time to follow up on that good fortune. A week or two following the convention, you should be sending a note and more samples to the professionals you met. Use the mail route to keep your name and your work fresh in their minds. Most publishers and editors have an extensive and busy convention travel circuit. They have neither the time nor the inclination to keep track of everyone or follow through with them the minute they return to their offices. By using the mail, you ensure that you are remembered, and even considered for upcoming projects.

Although one of the first steps in making your presence known as an aspiring pro is to send samples of your work, with an introductory letter, to editors and publishers with whom you'd like to work, the question to keep in mind at all times is: "Has my work reached a sufficiently professional level?" If you feel your work stands up to the quality of workmanship currently being handled by a publisher you wish to approach, then send your samples. The best possible result from sending an unsolicited mail submission would be that the publisher sees your stuff, loves it, and contacts you immediately with work. The worst case scenario is that they reject you soundly, and admonish you to consider another career. However, it's most likely, if you follow the proper procedure and etiquette for mail-in samples, you will get a polite—and sometimes encouraging—acknowledgment that your samples were received, and will be "kept on file." Don't be discouraged. Getting a response of this nature should be considered reassuring. It indicates there is some interest, and if you follow through diligently and reliably by all available avenues, that interest could ultimately blossom into a real job offer.

Be incredibly tenacious. I think that we are fortunate in comics to have a system where eventually talent wins out. If you really do have the talent, if you know how to tell an entertaining story, if you have the tools—writing comics is really a unique form of writing, and you need those tools—and you are willing to work wherever you can possibly get work, I think you'll persevere.

DAN JURGENS
Writer/Artist

What Mail System Should I Use?

There are a number of mail systems available to you, including couriers like Federal Express (FedEx) and United Parcel Service (UPS). However, be forewarned; the correct procedure for sending unsolicited samples and introductory letters to a publisher is to use the regular postal service. Although a courier service can often get your material there much quicker, it is considered inappropriate to use this method for submitting new work for consideration. In addition, you are looking at costs that are astronomically higher than is truly feasible, if you are contacting several publishers regularly.

There are some things you should do to ensure that your system for sending out materials is streamlined and efficient.

1. Familiarize Yourself with the System.

Take a trip to your local post office. Talk to a postal worker and find out about the different types of mail classes available to you. Ask about approximate delivery times for your target cities, so you can better estimate the time to allow before following up on a submission.

2. Stock Up on Mailing Supplies.

While at the post office, invest in a few items. First, get a postage rate schedule, which is free for the asking, and provides a good reference in your home or office. With a postage rate schedule you can figure out the correct postage for small packages you're sending out. It will also help you calculate the correct postage required for self-addressed, stamped envelopes (SASE), which should be included with all submissions.

It is also worth investing in an inexpensive postage scale. You can pick these up at any office supply store or through mail order catalogues. With the scale and the postal rate schedule, you will save yourself countless trips to the post office, and make your regular submissions procedures much more efficient. This will ultimately leave you time to do what you enjoy most—practice and hone your writing skills.

With the thought in mind of conserving time wasted on multiple trips to the post office, you should also seriously consider investing $15 to $20 in postage stamps to keep on hand. The best way to calculate how much you should have convenient is to make up a submissions package and determine the postage required using your rate schedule and scale.

If you decide to purchase a stock of stamps, have the post office give you an assortment of denominations that you can mix and match as required. Keep your postage in a clean dry storage area (separate envelopes for each denomination is a good organizational practice) to ensure you don't spend an afternoon steaming apart gummed-together stamps. Unfortunately, I learned this the hard way my first year in sunny, humid Florida!

Besides postage materials, you should also invest in a package of plain manila envelopes. These can be acquired many places but shop around, since prices can vary greatly. Avoid the urge to use brightly colored or decorated envelopes, although you can utilize your business card logo if you have one. Although flashy packaging may seem like it would be better for catching the eye of a potential employer, what it will really say is that you (a) are spending too much time doing silly things instead of honing your skills and (b) haven't yet learned correct professional business procedures. There's a humorous old principle called KISS: Keep It Simple, Stupid. This precept is a very good philosophy to follow when handling any type of business, including mail submissions.

When you purchase your envelopes, remember to stick with the standard 9" x 12" size. Always send writing submissions flat. Do not fold them letter-style—this is considered poor business form.

Also, remember to buy some standard legal size envelopes (No. 10s) to use for SASEs.

John Moore, Writer
Credits Include: *American Flagg! Vol #2* from First Comics;
Superboy, Ironwolf: Fires of the Revolution (with Howard Chaykin),
Batman/Houdini: The Devil's Workshop (with Chaykin), *Under a
Yellow Sun: A Novel by Clark Kent* from DC Comics; *Doom 2099,
X-Men 2099, X-Men Unlimited, X-Factor* from Marvel Comics. TV
series work includes Executive Story Consultant for *The Flash* (with
Chaykin) and writing episodes of *Human Target, The Palace Guard*
(with Chaykin), and *Viper*.

Question: Are there any specific approaches you would suggest that
new writers take for breaking into comics?

I have gotten most of my work from phone contact and I didn't really solicit
work through the mail. It has all been solicited either in person at conventions or
publishers offices, or following up on contacts with editors by phone.

Mail follow up is very important, even though my circumstances were such
that I was offered more work than I really had to actively seek. For a newcomer
though, you definitely need to follow up, because when you talk to an editor
he/she is usually busy with a number of different things and it's better to follow
up by mail. Not just to give him/her something to add to the pile of work on
his/her desk, but to remind him/her of who you are. There's so much distraction
for editors in most cases that they need "big neon signs" to remind them of the
people who are, for the moment, on the periphery.

For a writer, it's difficult to send in a mail submission, because you can't
expect an editor to really read that much material. They rarely have time to read
submissions, unless it's something they've specifically requested. If you have
done any work at all—an independent comic, or for a small publisher—send that
along. Send copies of your published work. It doesn't really make sense to send
copies of prose to a comic book editor, because it doesn't show that you know
how to write comics. If you're going to be bold, and submit plot ideas—which I
can't guarantee any editor has time to read—keep them brief. A paragraph for a
story idea is more than enough, because an editor is not going to have time to
read anymore. And if he likes the idea, he'll get in touch with you and ask for
more. Don't do a huge amount of work—you can't expect an editor to examine a
large unsolicited document.

There's no question that it's a good idea to have an artist illustrate a new
writer's scripting. If there's any comics work that a writer can show—actual

words and pictures, even if it's not published—it has a better chance of being examined. You need to convince an editor that you can tell comic book stories in comic book form, and you can't do that by prose.

Also, a lot of breaking in has to do with being in the right place at the right time. Make yourself known to editors. Also, if you're really driven to do comics, you just have to find a way to do it. You may not get financial remuneration immediately, but I definitely believe in the "do-it-yourself" ethic. There are a lot of people who started doing small press, photocopied mini-comics, like Matt Feazell and Peter Bagge, which led to higher visibility work. It's a way to simply do it, instead of waiting around for somebody to discover you, because there's no guarantee that you're going to be "picked out of the air" or that somebody is just going to recognize your talent. Sometimes people are lucky and that happens, but otherwise the best thing to do is just work at it in some way.

Art from Ironwolf: Fires of the Revolution

3. Organize Your Own Mail-Out System

Once you decide to begin sending out samples, you should have an organized method for proceeding. This will ensure two things: that you send regularly to publishers without accidentally doubling up or omitting one, and that you have a record of who got what and when.

One way of tracking your mail submissions is to keep a log and file system. This means keeping a file folder on each publisher. In each folder, keep any notes you might have on that publisher (your contacts, their responses, etc.) and copies of any samples you have sent.

Your log should be a notebook, another file folder, or even a computer file. It should contain the details about what you sent, to whom it was sent, and when it was sent. You should also note what the submissions package contained, the amount of postage you used, when or if you received a response, and any additional comments you might have about the entry. This type of log may seem excessively organized, but if you're frequently sending out multiple submissions, this allows you to track to whom you have sent what, when, and how much it cost you. You will be able to balance your investment in the various companies against the responses you get from them. It will let you add or delete possible employers, and make changes in the actual contact person. It will also allow you to keep track of when to send updated samples and to whom you should direct them.

There are many other ways of tracking your mail submissions. If the log and file system doesn't work for you, then develop one that does. Just keep in mind, if you begin to practice good business skills at this early stage, not only will this help you down the road when you've established yourself professionally, but it will also serve to impress upon the publisher that you are a serious, competent, and reliable business person. In combination with good creative skills, this may make the difference for you getting the job over someone who is just as skilled, but who may show less professional prowess.

What Should I Be Sending?

In Chapter One, I outlined the procedure for getting the submissions guidelines for each company. Additionally, Appendix D at the back of this book provides the actual submissions guidelines for various publishers. Once you have received that information, and you've organized your mail-out system, the next step is to decide what you should be sending. This is determined by a variety of factors, including to whom you are sending, what type of work you're doing and whether this is a first-time, unsolicited contact.

If this is a "cold" or first-time, unsolicited submission, then the package you send should include samples of your work, as outlined by the company's submissions guidelines as well as an introductory cover letter and a business card. You should also make sure to include a SASE for a response (see box on page 87 for which elements the two types of cover letters should include).

If you are following up on a previous meeting—for example, from a convention or store appearance—your sample package should reflect this. If your first contact was

COVER LETTER GUIDELINES

A First-Time Submissions Cover Letter

- Keep your letter brief, typed, and follow business letter format.

- Include your contact information: full name, address, and phone number.

- Introduce yourself (e.g., "I am a 20-year-old college student. . . .")

- Provide a brief description of related education and work experience.

- Describe your specific work interests and willingness to continually work at improving your skills.

- Conclude with a courteous salutation.

- Be patient in awaiting a response.

A Follow-Up Contact Cover Letter

- Follow the same basic format as for the first-time submissions cover letter but include reference to your previous meeting (e.g., "I was delighted to meet you at the HeroesCon two weeks ago, and appreciated the time you took to look at my work.")

- Include a brief explanation for this follow up (e.g., "I just wanted to send you copies of my most recent samples for your consideration.")

- Keep the tone of your letter friendly, but businesslike. Avoid taking an overly familiar tone.

simply voiced interest, then treat this as a first-time submission but mention your meeting with the editor in your cover letter. On the other hand, if you had the opportunity to give the editor a business card or left samples with that editor, then your first contact has been made and now you should simply follow up as a courtesy. Send additional copies of any samples you may have presented in person, assuming that the editor might have misplaced them in his or her travels. This will ensure that you are not accidentally swept under the rug. If you have new, improved samples, then enclose these with the copies, or in place of the samples you initially provided. Again, include another business card and a SASE for the editor's convenience.

For follow-up contact, your cover letter can take a slightly more personal tone, but DO NOT assume that you have been burned into that editor's memory, or that you are suddenly best buddies! This is still a potential employer for whom you hope to work. Treat this person with that respect. It's always best to assume that you aren't remembered.

Providing the editor with a reference point and reintroducing yourself is a professional courtesy.

Keep in mind, these people are meeting and doing business with thousands of individuals each year. If they only met you once, briefly, at a convention, it is most likely that you will have to jog their memory. They will appreciate the reminder, and you will impress them with your professional expertise. That will help to get you noticed.

Who Should Receive Your Samples

Your writing samples are essentially your job application. Therefore, you should direct them to the companies with whom you wish to gain employment. If your interests lie exclusively with superhero subject matter, then you should restrict your mail-outs to the mainstream companies like DC Comics, Marvel Comics, Image Comics, and Acclaim Comics. If your interests are a little more diverse or esoteric, then consider some smaller, independent publishers like Caliber Press, Dark Horse Comics, and Antarctic Press.

Whatever the material in which you are interested, just remember to send samples to a variety of editors representing that company, and to continue sending samples regularly and consistently. If you target only one editor, your samples may end up buried deep under a stack of other work. It may take months before your samples again see the light of day and by then they will be dated. But if you send them to more than one editor, they will have a greater chance of being seen, which will significantly improve your chances of getting work.

The editor is not there to give you a break. You're trying to sell him something. Try to imagine what it's like from his side of the desk, and give him something that'll make his job easier. If you can't deliver what he needs, then rethink what you're offering or find another editor. Railing against the stupidity of editors who can't understand why your work is perfect won't help you sell a thing.

KURT BUSIEK,
Writer

Which Editor Should I Target?

When sending out sample packages, it's important to do your homework. As I suggested in Chapter One, keeping a record of publishers and editors is very important. This will provide you with the information you need to decide who should be the target of your sample packages.

Some companies have a single New Submissions Editor. If they do, this information will most likely be specified in their submissions guidelines. In these cases, you should make sure that editor receives a sample package, in addition to targeting any specific book editors. Send packages to any editors who work on books you are interested in, or whose work has been associated with books you've enjoyed or believe to be successful.

Keep one important point in mind: Don't always expect to hear back from everyone you approach, SASE or not. Many editors will be too busy, not interested, or might even be short on professional etiquette of their own. But don't give up. Keep sending out those samples.

When Should I Send My Samples?

Once you have selected the companies you wish to approach, and the specific editors you wish to target, then you should begin sending out your samples regularly. A good rule is to send new material every six to eight weeks. This shows both your sincere interest and your dedication, and will allow the editors to track your improvement. Additionally, by sending sample packages at regular intervals, you make your name a recognizable quantity in the office. "Here come Joe Pro's samples, just like clockwork!" Then, when a job comes up where they need someone new, or quickly, Joe Pro's name is still on their mind, and he's got himself a job.

Keep a few important points in mind though:

1. *Don't make a pest of yourself.* If you're always sending the same stuff, and don't pay attention to any critical feedback from the editor, it will only serve to alienate them—a guarantee that you won't get work. Try to leave a reasonable time span between submissions. If you send stuff in too frequently, you'll just annoy the editors by adding to their already overwhelming workload.

2. *Don't be too familiar in your correspondence.* If you try to be too buddy-buddy, you may lose a shot at a professional job. Also, try to avoid the "gushing" fan letters, which do nothing to illustrate your professional skills, and only serve to irritate the editor since they run into that all the time at conventions!

3. *Be sure to reintroduce yourself each time you send samples.* No matter how often you send in submissions, don't assume that you are so memorable that everyone will know who you are the instant they see your name. Remember, these people are looking at hundreds of unsolicited submissions, and many of them have been in the slush pile for extended periods of time. Additionally, they must consider all the material from established pros looking for more work. Remind them who you are, when you last sent samples, and what they were. This way, they'll have a reference point, and can quickly locate you in the submissions file if they choose.

4. *Don't be demanding.* Despite how often you've sent sample packs, or whether you've ever received a response, don't be surly, demanding, or issue an ultimatum in your correspondence. If you feel that your work is going unacknowledged, consider sending your samples to a different editor. Your target editor may be too busy to deal with unsolicited material, or may be too unassertive to send you a rejection. Always keep the tone of your correspondence respectful and polite.

   Remember, they're doing you a favor by looking at your material; you're not doing them a favor by sending them your samples. If you're dissatisfied with their response, consider sending a simple, polite note with your next sample submission. State that you will be available for future work and then make it your last submission to that editor.

5. *Keep target editors informed of your employment status.* Just because Editor A hires you before Editor B, doesn't mean that you won't ever get work with Editor B. Drop Editor B a note with updated material—perhaps once or twice a year—and mention

any professional jobs you do find, accompanied by a copy of the published material. This will show your "hireability" and reliability as a freelancer. Nothing encourages employers more than knowing someone else thinks you're worth hiring!

Also, just because you get one professional comic job, doesn't guarantee your career is set. A noteworthy characteristic of being a freelancer is the need to constantly pursue new work, line up leads on new jobs and promote yourself. You'll have to work hard at staying regularly employed, so make sure you keep your contacts with various editors alive.

ProFile

Mark Evanier, Writer
Credits Include: Assistant to Jack Kirby; *Blackhawk, New Gods* (Writer/Co-Creator) from DC Comics; *DNAgents, Crossfire* from Eclipse; *Hollywood Superstars* from Epic/Marvel; *The Mighty Magnor* from Malibu Comics; *Groo The Wanderer* (with Sergio Aragones) from Image Comics; *Yogi Bear, Scooby-Doo, Bugs Bunny, Flintstones,* and *Daffy Duck* from Gold Key Comics; *Mickey Mouse, Super Goof* from Disney. Some of his TV credits include *Welcome Back Kotter, Cheers, Bob, Love Boat, Garfield and Friends, Mother Goose and Grimm, ABC Weekend Special, Dungeons & Dragons,* and *Scooby-Doo.*

Question: You've worked in the industry for a long time, and have surely seen a lot of monumental changes. Is there anything that you feel is noteworthy to mention? What change has impressed you the most? Depressed you the most?

What has depressed me the most has been the continual narrowing of our audience down to where so many publishers don't think you can sell anything but superheroes. Who would ever have thought we'd see the day when Donald Duck would be an "alternative" comic? What has impressed me the most have been the gains in creative rights. Back in the seventies, there were a lot of us lobbying for things like royalty plans, reprint fees, creator-owned titles, return of original art, etc. Some of us had to endure some pretty brutal assaults by company reps who were dead-set determined that these things would never happen, could never happen, that we were idiots for thinking a company could return original art and not go bankrupt, etc. I am still stunned by how fast one company man went from insulting those who suggested royalty plans made sense to taking credit for his company's new royalty plan. (And I suppose, to some extent, it has depressed me that these breakthroughs took place too late for pioneers like Jack Kirby and Wally Wood to fully reap the benefits of their genius.)

The Response Card—A SASE Alternative

If you don't require that your writing samples be returned, save on postage by including a response card instead of a SASE. The SASE will require a minimum of a first-class letter stamp, whereas a response card only needs postcard postage. That savings can add up pretty quickly as postage for additional submission packages.

A response card takes a little bit of work to design, but can be quite valuable. Simply, it is a postcard that lists preprinted responses an editor can check off, and a comment box. There are many benefits to this method, but most importantly it provides the editor with an inexpensive, quick, and easy way to acknowledge receipt of your material. This is particularly useful if they are simply updating your file. If they wish to contact you for a job, they will follow through independently. In addition, if you note the publisher information on the card when you address it, you can keep a detailed record of responses, and any comments they may take the time to note. The response card shows your commitment to the business aspects of working as a freelancer, and will not go unnoticed by the editor.

PERSONAL INTERVIEWS

Personal interviews are not the most useful of the methods available for securing writing work in the comics industry. In general, publishers and editors tend to only schedule interviews for artists who wish to have their portfolios reviewed. Because reviewing writing samples requires a lot of concentration, it is rare that a publisher will schedule an interview to look at writing samples.

However, anything is worth a try. Any personal connection you can make with a publisher increases your chances of being considered for future work. Sometimes being in the right place at exactly the right time can mean the difference between obscurity and employment. If you are a committed, businesslike individual with the work skills necessary for getting the job done, and if you follow the correct procedures for securing an interview, the personal interview could be a valuable tool.

Scheduling a Personal Interview

There is no simple little trick or piece of advice that will secure you this elusive prize. To get a personal interview, you must do a lot of hard work, plenty of preparation, and invest much time and energy. Your best shot at an interview will manifest itself if you've followed the recommended steps of preparing your samples, attending conventions to make professional contacts, and sending out samples by mail. One or all these techniques can open up the opportunity to approach a particular editor or publisher at their offices—sometimes even at their request. However, this route may not appeal to everyone.

I would suggest that writers read everything they can get their hands on—newspapers, magazines, fiction, non-fiction, and comics. A good writer writes what they know, so the more you know the more you can write effectively.

JOE PRUETT
Writer/Editor

If you think you have enough talent and business savvy, and you are fortunate enough to be conveniently located near the publisher you are targeting, then you probably could take advantage of the interview process without the preliminary steps I've recommended. Keep in mind, though, that the preparation of your samples is very critical to a personal interview. Also, making connections in person at conventions, and through mail submissions, can establish a friendlier, more familiar and relaxed interview setting.

Most publishers have regularly scheduled interview/portfolio-review days and times. If you wish to pursue an interview uninvited, it is in your best interest to call ahead and find out when these activities are scheduled, and if they will interview prospective writers. If they do interview writers, you should always make an appointment. This is an indicator of your professionalism. To simply show up at the publisher's office requesting (or worse yet, demanding) a personal interview is the ultimate in rudeness and inconsiderate business practice. It will do nothing but damage your newly developing career, and alienate you with that particular company.

Assuming you've followed all the steps necessary to reach your goal of a personal interview, and provided you have the means to reach the publisher's office in person, there are a number of things you should consider to ensure you make a good impression, including good preparation, personal presentation and proper interview etiquette.

- *Prepare properly for your interview.* This preparation can take a variety of forms. It is important to be familiar with the following information: the company history and their published works, the segment of the market they tend to target, their use of new talent, the editorial staff and their credits, and how your work will fit into their publishing line.

- *Familiarize yourself with the publisher and their products.* If you want to create comics then you should be familiar with that product, how it's produced and by whom. This does not mean you should learn the names of every book or character the company produces so you can try to impress your interviewer by reciting that information. It means familiarizing yourself with the books they are promoting heavily, any works that have produced accolades or attention for the company, and most important, books on which you would be interested in working.

  I cannot emphasize this point enough: If you are set on working on a particular book you must be familiar with the character, its background and history, and what material is currently being published on that character. It is not in your best interest to show up at the interview, say, "I really want to work on Batman, and I've got this totally cool idea . . ." and then have the interviewer look at you astounded, and tell you "We just did that story two months ago! Don't you read the book?" This would be bad. Very bad.

  Learn about the characters, books, and company that you are pursuing. Knowledge and good preparation can be very powerful tools.

- *Don't be a geek.* Sorry to be so harsh, but there are certain behaviors that are completely unacceptable for an aspiring pro. Sure, it's exciting and wonderful that you

Dan Jurgens, Writer/Artist

Credits Include: *Warlord* (drawing), *Superman* (writing & drawing), *Zero Hour* mini-series (writing & drawing), *Justice League* (writing & drawing), *Green Arrow* (drawing), *Flash Gordon* mini-series (writing & drawing), *Booster Gold* (created, writing & drawing) from DC Comics; *Superman/Aliens* special (writing & drawing, with inks by Kevin Nowlan) from DC Comics and Dark Horse Comics.

Question: Do you believe a personal interview can be beneficial for a new writer trying to acquire work in the comics business?

I think that it is obviously beneficial, but I don't expect an interview will actually get you "the job." Writing jobs in comics are the hardest to come by for newcomers. An editor can look at samples from a new artist, and within five seconds know if that artist has the tools to do the job. By and large, if you look at where the writers come from, they are generally from one of about three sources: artists who convince an editor to give them a chance to write, assistant editors who convince an editor to give them a chance to write, or they are established writers who started out working with the independents and got noticed and just kept moving up through the ranks somehow. There are some writers who have worked in other industries and crossed over, but generally that tends to be for very specific stuff, such as the *Star Trek* books. I don't think we're an industry that works with any great intent, or by great design, to find writers from other fields and bring them into comics. It happens, but it's usually by association.

Jurgen's art from Superman #82

Neil Gaiman, Writer

Credits Include: *Black Orchid, Death: The High Cost of Living, Sandman* series and collections, *Violent Cases, Mr. Punch, The Last Temptation* from DC Vertigo; *Signal to Noise* (illustrated by Dave McKean) from Gollancz and Dark Horse Comics; *Miracleman: The Golden Age* from Eclipse and Harper Collins; *Angels and Visitations* (prose) from DreamHaven.

Question: Is there anything you specifically recommend that writing newcomers avoid doing when trying to get work in comics?

It's too easy for newcomers to do what they think their editors would like to see, not what they want to do—to imitate someone else's style, whether as a writer or as an artist, instead of finding their own voices. And your own voice is the only thing that makes you different, interesting, or, frankly, popular. Be yourself, not a pale shadow of someone else.

Art by Marc Hempel for
Sandman: The Kindly Ones

finally scored a personal interview. It could mean they think you've got some real potential. But now it's time to act like a professional. Do not recite every tidbit of trivia you know about the company, employees, creators, or books. And most important, don't go on about other publishers and their works—they really don't care what you think about their competitors. They're only interested in your knowledge about their company. Really.

• *Don't gush and fawn.* If you want to seem like a professional, then act like one. Sure, it's okay to be excited and enthusiastic. Many publishers are looking for that fresh outlook and new blood. They don't all want jaded cynics; they sometimes want open idealists. But if you can't stop going on about how faint you are from excitement, or that you "can't believe you're in the same room with the "famous editor/writer/artist" of a book you've been reading since you were born . . .," then you're going to lose out on a valuable opportunity—you won't even be considered for hiring, because they won't be convinced that you're serious about a professional career.

Just try to keep in mind that it's a job interview. Treat it like any other important job interview, and you'll have a much greater chance of success.

- *Examine the market the company targets.* If they are focusing on kids, then the samples you show them must be geared for that audience. If they are interested in the general mainstream audience, then it's unlikely they will be interested in your erotica samples.

- *Check if the publisher uses new talent.* Some companies make it a policy to limit new, unproven talent. Other companies make it a policy to regularly hire new, unproven talent. It's in your best interest to check out the published work of your target company to see where they stand on hiring newcomers. This will help provide you with some insight and guidance about whom you should aggressively approach, and who may require some extra groundwork and preparation.

- *Learn about the editorial staff and their credits.* Most people appreciate recognition for their work. Consequently, it doesn't hurt to familiarize yourself with the credits and credentials of the person who will be interviewing you. If it is a creator or editor whose work you are already familiar with, great! If their name is less familiar to you, then do a bit of research at your local comic shop, and find out what books they've been involved with, and whether they have any awards or special accolades to their credit. You may discover things about your interviewer that will provide you with some common ground, or give you a bit of extra confidence for your interview.

   This can also be a useful technique, if the interviewer is involved with any books on which you are interested in working. Your familiarity with material they are regularly involved with will impress upon them both your professional knowledge of the industry and your interest in their work.

- *Be sure your work fits into the company line.* If you tend to work very stylistically and create non-traditional comic art and writing, then you should be aware of what types of work the company produces. If they exclusively publish standard, mainstream superheroes, then it is unlikely that your alternative work will be of interest to them. Likewise, if you don't even have any interest in standard superhero material, then there's no real reason to interview with the company.

Personal Presentation

At last, you have finished researching your interviewer and the company. Your samples are organized and you're ready to go, right? Wrong. There's more. Although for some of you, this section may seem gratuitous—possibly even insulting—for others, this section may make the difference between being seriously considered a professional and never being interviewed again.

   What does personal presentation mean? It means personal hygiene, the way you dress, your mannerisms, and how you speak. I'm not here to provide you with a charm school education, but I do want you to consider a few important aspects of personal presentation that are considered by all interviewers when they sit down with a new job candidate.

Although it may sound simplistic and discriminatory, your personal hygiene will significantly influence the outcome of your interview. Clean, combed hair, brushed teeth, bathing, and deodorant are essentials. Sorry to get personal, but these are frequently mentioned points of contention with many hiring professionals. If your interviewer is badly distracted by your powerful body odor, your interview will be hurried and leave a markedly unpleasant impression, despite your overwhelming talents. Take the time prior to leaving for your interview to ensure that you've been meticulous about your personal appearance and cleanliness.

The way you dress goes hand in hand with personal hygiene. There is no point in spending time cleaning yourself up if you plan to dress in the same dirty clothes you've worn for the past week. Clean clothes are also an essential part of personal hygiene.

The type of clothes you wear isn't quite as important for a freelancer interviewing for work, as it might be for an office worker. But to make a good impression, a neat, clean appearance is essential. Don't wear clothes that are in disrepair or badly worn out, just because they're your favorites or have always been lucky. You'll just make a bad impression. On the other hand, a freelancer who shows up in a tux and tails will make just as bad an impression. Dress appropriately, neatly, and in a businesslike way. Casual is okay, but this doesn't mean sloppy jeans and a faded, dirty T-shirt.

Oh, and don't show up for an interview with Company A wearing clothing sporting the logo of Company B! If you insist on wearing logo-covered clothing, make sure it's Company A's!

Good manners don't come naturally to everyone, but they should. Respect, consideration and courtesy are the foundation of good business relations. Be polite—not just with the interviewer, but with the secretary, the receptionist, and any other individuals you meet. Practice good manners in your day-to-day life, and it will come naturally in your interview. Good manners include the following:

- Call ahead to arrange your interview, don't just show up and expect to be seen.

- Leave your full name and contact information when you make your appointment.

- Learn and use the names of the secretary/receptionist and your interviewer, but err toward the formal side (Ms. Bastienne, Mr. Reed) rather than the familiar side.

- Be punctual. Show up a few minutes before your appointment time, and politely notify the secretary/receptionist that you have arrived. This responsible behavior is one indication that you can handle deadlines and assignments.

- Sit quietly and patiently until you are called. Your politeness will invite a professional response.

- Make eye contact and shake hands firmly. When you are met by your interviewer, thank them for seeing you, and be open and friendly. In doing so you will help set the tone of the interview and make a positive impression.

Joe R. Lansdale, Writer

Credits Include: *Jonah Hex: Two Gun Mojo, Jonah Hex: Riders of the Worm, Blood and Shadows* (artist, Mark Nelson) from DC Comics; *The Lone Ranger: It Crawls* from Topps Comics; *Tarzan's Lost Adventure* from Dark Horse Comics; *Mucho Mojo* (novel), *Two Bear Mambo* (novel), *Savage Season* (novel), *Cold in July* (novel) from Mysterious Press; *Writer of the Purple Rage* (short story collection) from CD Publications; *Batman: Captured by the Engines* from Warner Books.

Question: Do you believe that hiring an agent is beneficial for writers? Would you recommend this practice to newcomers?

I think one thing that a comic book writers needs, which I'm sure the industry is not excited about them having, is an agent. I think writers need somebody who really knows what they're doing. They need the equivalent of a literary agent. My literary agent handles my comic book contracts.

I think that the comic book publishers are, in many ways, a lot more professional with their contracts and getting business done than the book publishers. But the comic book publishers control a lot more of the ownership rights. Of course, if you're working on *Batman*—it's theirs! Everybody ought to realize that going in. I hear so many people whine and complain about some project they got into and I say to them, "Well, you knew *Swamp Thing* (for example) wasn't yours when you started, didn't you?"

On the other hand, I do believe that better contracts could be established if there were agents who were really professional—not just people who mail a few things around—but agents who are really professional. Primarily literary agents who are also willing to handle comic book contracts.

- When asked, state clearly and concisely what you believe the purpose of the interview to be, and what your goal is.

- Answer questions politely, honestly, openly and with good humor (that doesn't mean crack jokes!).

- Don't interrupt the interviewer or drone on incessantly about unrelated personal matters or thoughts. Do listen carefully to what is said.

- At the end of the interview, regardless of your perception of the outcome, thank your interviewer for his/her time. Also don't forget to thank the secretary/receptionist as you leave.

In all exchanges, keep in mind how you would feel if your positions were reversed, and imagine the manner in which you would want to be spoken to. Let good sense and common courtesy dictate your manners.

The way you speak is closely linked with your manners, but is important enough to merit mention on its own. The way you speak can influence the behavior of those around you. Use proper English and avoid slang, expletives and fashionable terminology. Make your statements and questions clear and concise, and you will avoid confusion and misunderstandings. Don't try to be "cool," just try to be sincere, polite, and enthusiastic. And be yourself; a contrived personality is transparent, irritating, and could negatively affect the outcome of your interview.

Interview Etiquette

Interview etiquette is closely related to good manners, and the one rarely occurs without the other. By interview etiquette, I refer to the way in which you conduct yourself in the interview—which behaviors are acceptable and expected, and which will ruin your chances of gaining employment.

In the previous section on manners, I listed some items that also fall under the heading of interview etiquette. In addition to those aspects of interview etiquette, here is a list of Do's and Don'ts you should familiarize yourself with before you go in.

Don'ts

Don't compare your interviewer, their company, or any of their published work to their competitor(s). Focus on them—they're the one interviewing you!

Don't ever criticize another creator's work. You're there to be interviewed, not provide a critique. This is guaranteed to make a very bad impression.

Don't think for one second that your "massive talent" will carry your lack of professional organization because it won't!

Don't prepare a list of requests or demands—this will only guarantee you won't be hired.

Don't memorize the company's complete published works and then recite them to your interviewer.

Don't go in with a negative, arrogant, or know-it-all attitude. It's a job interview. You need to make a good impression.

Do's

Do organize your writing samples in a professional and easy-to-read manner.

Do put together a sample package you can leave with your interviewer, including a business card.

Do list the types of characters and/or books on which you'd like to work, and be prepared to describe this to the interviewer.

Do prepare yourself to accept other material/assignments if they're offered. After all, you have to start somewhere!

Do go in with a positive, friendly and enthusiastic outlook.

WORKING FOR A PUBLISHER

By and large, the most reliable way of becoming a freelance comics writer is to gain experience, expertise, knowledge, and social contacts in the comics industry. The best way of obtaining all those things is to work for a publisher.

Many of the top comics writers in our industry spent at least some time working for a publisher in some capacity. Many started out as editorial assistants, and moved up through the ladder to managing and group editors. Some of our best known writers still work for a publisher while maintaining a part-time freelance career, with much satisfaction. When most comics writers and editors are asked, they will confidently answer that working in a publishing house is immensely beneficial to an aspiring writer's freelance career.

The Benefits of Working for a Publisher

Working for a publisher provides a wide range of benefits, both professionally and personally. On the personal level, you will have a steady, paying job with all the benefits (health coverage, retirement plans, proven employment credit record, etc.) associated with regular employment. That security can offer an aspiring writer a lot of freedom to pursue writing work at his or her own speed, without the constant need to search for work in order to pay the bills.

On a professional level, working for a publisher provides you with a relative bonanza of benefits, including gains in experience and industry knowledge, social contacts, and exposure to new projects.

One of the most valuable aspects of working for a publisher is the industry experience a writer can gain. You will become well versed in the way the industry and publishing houses operate, in how a comic book is put together, and in all the technical ins-and-outs necessary to comics publishing. That knowledge will serve you well in your comics writing career, by familiarizing you with inside information unavailable to your freelance competitors.

In addition to the connections you will make at the publisher where you work—with editors, production people, and management—you will also form relationships with other creators (both writers and artists) and employees of other publishing houses. Each of these relationships can serve to advance your freelance writing career through connections to new projects, potential creative team-ups, and possible employment positions with other publishers. These contacts can benefit you while you are still employed with a publisher, and can also pave the way to new professional ties if you decide to go freelance full-time.

As an employee of a publisher, you will have creative opportunities many freelancers will never enjoy. Depending on the publisher, and your work responsibilities, you may have first shot at many new projects being developed or be given the opportunity to develop new projects for that publisher. Additionally, if your publisher is one permitting simultaneous freelance work (some publishers require exclusive agreements from employees), you may have improved chances of acquiring work projects from other publishers due to the recognition factor associated with your name as a publisher employee, or due to social contacts you will have established.

Your Transition to Freelancer

If after a period of time working for a publisher you choose to go full-time as a freelancer, each of the benefits listed above will apply to the new direction in your career. Your expertise, social contacts, and exposure to new projects will all help in your comics writing pursuits. Additionally, if you maintain an amicable relationship with your former employer and co-workers, this can also represent some very lucrative opportunities, in the form of new projects.

Get a contract—get everything in writing. And try to understand that you are fulfilling an agreement. A lot of the problems with late books these days are due to the fact that the artists and writers don't turn in their work on time. In our business you have to turn in your work on time otherwise there's a domino effect because every other member of the creative team is affected by your delays.

CLYDENE NEE
Colorist and Graphic Designer

Jobs in Comics Publishing and How to Get Them

If you choose to search for work with a publisher, there are a variety of jobs available. Regardless of the position you choose to pursue, the process of acquiring the job is the same as in many other businesses—you must apply for a position, then interview. However, unlike other businesses there are a number of ways of getting your foot in the door for consideration.

Tactics for seeking a job with a publisher include writing an inquiry letter, filling out a job application, and making contact through conventions. It is convention contact that distinguishes our business from many other industries. At conventions, publishers are often on the look out for new folks to hire for their staff. They can be receptive to applicants, and have even been known to conduct informal interviews. This is one of the areas where social connections can help you. By making solid social contacts with a publisher, you may find that your chances of acquiring a job with them are greatly improved.

Publishing jobs that can be of some benefit to comics writers include advertising and marketing, office help, and editorial. Although the first two can be helpful, the most beneficial jobs are in the editorial department. Editors are expected to assume a variety of responsibilities. They are assigned, or may choose, the variety of projects they oversee to completion. The editor is expected to be the quality-control person and the primary communication link in the comic-publishing chain.

Editors often have to seek out talent for the projects under their auspices. They act as the communication intermediary between the creator and the company. They examine and edit the stories and art produced for a particular project and oversee its transit through the various company departments. Editors control the processing of the paperwork for contracts and payments to freelancers. They have a say in the promotion of the product by giving input to the advertising department about what fans will respond to. They also have contact with the distributors and work at conventions. The editor advises the company about whom should be rehired for future projects, and makes suggestions for new projects. Depending on the temperament and policies of the company, the editor may also be given creative opportunities as a writer.

Editorial department jobs include editorial assistants, assistant editors, editors, group editors (oversee a group of editors in addition to managing their own books), specialty editors (i.e., licensing, characters, collections, new submissions, etc.), managing editors, and executive editors. As in any other business, unless you come into the company with extensive education, expertise, or experience, you will be expected to work your way up from the bottom.

CHAPTER FIVE

HOW TO BE A GOOD BUSINESSPERSON

Now that you have finally secured that long, sought-after job in the comics industry, there are a number of things that you must keep in mind to ensure that you conduct yourself as a good businessperson. Raw talent is not sufficient to maintain a professional career. You must master basic business skills.

Many of the skills that are necessary to assure your status as a comics professional are simple, yet often overlooked or ignored. By demonstrating your abilities as a businessperson, you also demonstrate to your publisher that you are a reliable source for good work.

You will need to master many aspects of legal techniques, bookkeeping, general office organization, communication abilities, business responsibilities, office technology, and self-promotion. In essence, you have to become a one-person business operation. Having these business skills will go a long way toward advancing your comics career.

THE LEGAL ASPECTS OF BUSINESS

There are many legal aspects to working as a professional in the comics industry. You must have a good understanding of negotiations, contracts, copyrights, ownership of original works, licensing, and standard business forms. Each of these areas is in itself a complex topic, but with a few basics, you can get a reasonable start on being a good businessperson.

Negotiations

In order to agree on the basic terms of the contract, and still be sure to accommodate each other's needs, the writer and publisher representatives must sit down together and negotiate the work agreement. The purpose of this negotiation is not to defeat the other, but for each party to feel that its needs have been satisfied. An editor must decide whether the work to be provided by the writer will suit the needs of the project, and will fall within the financial budget, and must also ensure that the writer can meet the project deadlines. The writer, like any businessperson, must cover his or her overhead and make enough profit to live on, as well as gain creative satisfaction from the project. Therefore, the more information each party has about the other, the more effective the negotiation.

Anything on a contract is negotiable, even the date. And the size of the company has no real relationship to its business ethics...

NEIL GAIMAN
Writer

If the writer can determine ahead of time the standard pay for work with that specific company, then the writer will be better able to calculate a reasonable asking price. The editor's offer will be constrained by company guidelines and project restrictions, so any information he or she has about the writer's business requirements will help the negotiations go smoothly. If either the writer or the editor is unable or unwilling to meet the needs of the other, the negotiation will fail and the editor or writer may seek a contract elsewhere.

To ensure that negotiations are conducted fairly, it is important for you as a writer to approach the situation armed with knowledge. Familiarize yourself with the standard contractual agreement used by the company. Also, secure a copy of Fair Practice Guidelines for Freelancers (see Appendix C for legal reference books), to ensure you are informed about how negotiations should be conducted.

The negotiations will vary depending on how established you are as a writer in the comics industry. If you are a relative newcomer, negotiations will go quite differently than if you were an established pro, commanding some attention in the industry. As a new professional, you should listen carefully to what is offered, assess the value and desirability of the work contract, and make a decision. Don't dawdle in deciding, and be firm in your decisions. Often a newcomer will hurriedly accept a publishing agreement without familiarizing him or herself with the company's reputation. The urgency to be published blinds the new writer to the facts. There are many disreputable publishers who prey on naive newcomers. Your best defense is to be as informed about your work negotiations as possible. Do some research, make some phone calls. Get information from other professionals and newcomers. Ask a lot of questions. Only these things will keep you from becoming involved in a losing proposition.

Get it in writing.

DAVE GIBBONS
Writer/Artist

Contracts

A contract is by far the most important business aspect of becoming a professional. Do not forget this. No matter how badly you want to work and establish yourself, you just can't make a decent living by working for free. A bad contract can put you in an unpleasant situation—as can NO contract! A contract provides protection for both you and your employer. Both newcomers and established pros offer an astonishing number of story variations on being exploited by a publisher. It happens a lot in this industry. Because of the easy nature of the convention circuit and the related social angle, many "agreements" are formed casually over a drink at the bar—not particularly enforceable in a court of law!

Mark Evanier, Writer

Credits Include: Assistant to Jack Kirby; *Blackhawk*, *New Gods* (Writer/Co-Creator) from DC Comics; *DNAgents*, *Crossfire* from Eclipse; *Hollywood Superstars* from Epic/Marvel; *The Mighty Magnor* from Malibu Comics; *Groo The Wanderer* (with Sergio Aragones) from Image Comics; *Yogi Bear, Scooby-Doo, Bugs Bunny, Flintstones*, and *Daffy Duck* from Gold Key Comics; *Mickey Mouse, Super Goof* from Disney. Some of his TV credits include *Welcome Back Kotter, Cheers, Bob, Love Boat, Garfield and Friends, Mother Goose and Grimm, ABC Weekend Special, Dungeons & Dragons*, and *Scooby-Doo*.

Question: How much value do you place on written contracts, and the importance of creator-owned rights versus work-for-hire agreements?

Written contracts are important so there can be no quarrel later over what was was understood and agreed to. It is more—or, at least, equally—important to work with an entity you trust. I would not trust a written contract to protect me from someone I thought was deliberately trying to cheat me. But, even entering into a business arrangement with someone I trust, I'd want a contract first so that we don't become financially entwined and then start arguing over who promised what to whom. I should also add that the larger the company you're dealing with, the more important the written contract is, because the larger company goes through frequent changes of personnel, and it does little good to operate on a verbal understanding with someone who don't work there anymore.

Creator-owned rights are very important, especially if you're going to do something new. If you're doing the eight-zillionth *Spider-Man* story, it may not be as important, but every new creative project needs one ultimate voice behind it and it's better for that one voice on your character to be yours. I don't want to pour my guts into a character and then wake up one morning to find someone else has creative control of my hero and is remodeling him, expunging me and my views, painting over my canvas, as it were. Under work-for-hire, you concede all controls to the copyright holder who may not even read the thing, let alone understand it.

Art by Sergio Aragones from Groo The Wanderer

There are many different types of contract forms. They can be preprinted forms or specially typeset agreements. They can also be found in the fine print of purchase orders and payment invoice chits provided by the publisher. They can even be stamped on a payment check. Pay attention to what you're signing. It might just be your contract!

Work-for-Hire Contracts

According to copyright law, in a work-for-hire, the employer or other person for whom the work was prepared is considered the author for purposes of the title, and, unless the parties have expressly agreed otherwise in a written instrument signed by all parties, the employer or other person for whom the work was prepared owns all the rights comprised in the copyright.

Note that a work only becomes a work-for-hire when there is a signed (by both parties) written instrument expressly agreeing that the work is to be considered a work-for-hire. However, it is sometimes possible to reserve certain rights, such as the right to reproduce the work in other media. This should be considered when the negotiating is done.

In the comics industry, the work-for-hire contract (WFH)—also called a work-made-for-hire contract—is a double-edged sword. On the one hand, you are being offered the opportunity to work on an established character owned by a major company. This means that an established fan following most likely already exists for work produced around this character, and the potential for income generation and name recognition is great. Also, depending on your WFH contract, your royalties may help defer the cost of losing any rights to reprints of your work. On the other hand, you have lost any rights to republish your work elsewhere. Keep all of these issues in mind and know how much they matter to you before you sign all your rights away. (See Appendix B for an example of a WFH contract.)

Creator-Owned Rights Contracts

Another type of contract available in our business is the creator-owned rights contract (COR). For many writers, this is the contract of choice. Of all of the agreements you can negotiate with a publisher, this contract represents the most control for the writer. It provides that the writer is the sole author and owner of the material he or she creates, and lets he or she decide where, when, why, and how the work is reprinted.

However, the COR contract does not always guarantee immediate financial success. Sometimes the initial monies produced by a creator-owned property are small. But over time, and if the work is properly promoted, it can represent a substantial financial gain. At a later date the writer may also choose to sell all rights to the creation. That's fine, but remember they would never have had that right if the initial contract was a WFH agreement.

Basically, the COR agreement gives the writer more latitude and control than the WFH agreement. From a publisher's standpoint the WFH is more desirable, so you will find most major publishers use the WFH agreement. The COR agreement resides primarily with the smaller, creator-supportive independents. (See Appendix B for an example of a COR contract.)

There is great variety in the content of these contracts offering different rights and compensations. To find out more detail about contracts, check out some of the books noted on the reading list in Appendix C.

Before accepting work-for-hire assignments, weigh the value of your work-for-hire checks against a copyright certificate in your name. If the relatively short history of the comic book industry holds one lesson, it is to never underestimate the value of owning your own creation.

DENIS KITCHEN
Publisher, Kitchen Sink Press, Inc.

Contract Pointers

Before completing your contract negotiations and signing that all-important document, be sure to consider these points:

1.*Always, always, always have a written contract.* A contract does not necessarily have to

---

ProFile

Mike Baron, Comics Writer
Credits Include: *Nexus, Badger* for Dark Horse; *The Punisher* for Marvel; *Bruce Lee* for Malibu; *H.A.R.D. Corps* for Valiant.

Question: How much value do you place on written contracts and the importance of creator-owned rights versus work-for-hire agreements?

When it comes to written contracts, you have to take each situation as it comes. There are situations where a contract is not necessary, like when it's based on trust. But that's extremely rare. In general, I advise people to get a contract. Most of the companies for whom I work offer a pretty standard written contract, and they are reasonable people. I would advise anyone before they enter into a contract agreement to have a lawyer, or somebody with legal expertise, go over it and make sure that you get everything that you want.

When considering creator-owned rights versus work-for-hire agreements, it's really a trade-off. If you have a lot of talent, and you're offered the opportunity to work on a work-for-hire project with a high-profile character—such as *Punisher, Spider-Man,* or *Batman*—it would be foolish, especially early in your career, to pass that over. Those offers, however, are much more frequently given to artists, rather than writers. The reason for this is that it's just easier to get to know an artist's work. You can tell whether an artist has the right stuff in about 30 seconds of glancing through their portfolio. Whereas with a writer it's always best to see the writing in context before you can tell if you've got a "comer."

---

be in writing to be enforced, but this does not mean that a casual verbal agreement is easy to prove. There are a multitude of reasons for having a written contract, but the most important is that a contract protects both you and your employer's interests. It outlines, in black and white, the following specifics: the established deadlines, payment, royalties, complimentary copies of published work, who the copyright holder is, and any other features of the agreement. With the agreement in writing, these details are easy to refer to at any time during your work on the project. Simply put, it eliminates your questions, and serves as a written guide to what must be done, by whom and by what date, in exchange for what compensation.

2. *Read your contract.* Make sure that all the details that have been discussed are included in the written contract—right down to the number of free copies of the published work you should receive. If you don't outline it at the beginning, you may regret it in the end.

3. *Make sure both parties sign the contract.* Too simple? Apparently not, as there are many writers who neglect to turn in their signed contract until after the project has

---

There's nothing wrong with work-for-hire, if you know what you're getting into. These days it's not so bad, because the hard fights have all been won for us by the struggles of people like Jack Kirby and Frank Miller.

On the other hand, if you create something of value that you believe in, you should hang on to it, because you never know when you're going to catch lightning in a bottle. And that's what every creator dreams of: to come up with a character that's eminently marketable and hugely successful, from which he can gain the bulk of the receipts. And that only happens if you own it. It happened to [Kevin] Eastman and [Peter] Laird [creators of the *Teenage Mutant Ninja Turtles*], and to a degree it's happened for us with *Nexus*. But that's only through the good graces of Mike Richardson in a once-in-a-lifetime act, where he agreed to return copyright and trademark to us. Most people can't really count on that.

Art for Nexus: Into the Vortex *from Dark Horse Comics*

been completed, then protest futilely when an employer fails to honor their end of the bargain.

4. *Ensure that you get an original copy of the contract.* Two originals should be executed. The writer and the publisher should each get a copy of the original. If legal problems arise, do you really want to try to explain to your lawyer why you only have a photocopy, or worse yet, no copy at all?

5. *Make sure you understand all the language and items listed in your contract before you sign it.* Do not be overwhelmed by the language of your contract. If it is too difficult for you to wade through, first discuss it with the publisher. If they are unable or unwilling to simplify the language—or can't explain it to your satisfaction—then consider spending a nominal sum to have a lawyer look it over for you. Don't balk at the idea of the cost! Not all lawyers are costly, cutthroat, or inept. Most areas have a lawyer referral service, lawyers for the financially burdened, or a law school brimming with eager students. Use any of these avenues to have your contract deciphered. Don't sign it until you understand it, and are satisfied with the conditions.

COPYRIGHT

Copyright is a complex issue that we have already touched upon under the contract heading describing creator-owned rights. The ability for a writer to make a living is greatly dependent upon their ability to control the authorship of their work. In one sense, this degree of control is what sets the comics publishing market apart from other visual and print mediums. In our industry, many projects on which we are employed have already been "authored" by another creator. We are simply brought on board to continue to develop the property, i.e., continue the story. Under these circumstances, it is not unreasonable for the publisher to expect a creator to "work for hire." The publisher is technically the "author" of the materials on which you as a writer will work.

There are many critical details about copyright law in this country, and it is in your best interest as a creator, and a professional, to research how this information applies to you and protecting your career.

Copyright Notices

Copyright notices are a subject of great confusion. Unless you are working under a WFH contract, you should always put a copyright notice on all copies or publications of your original work, or see that the publisher does. The notice should start with the word "Copyright" or the copyright symbol © followed by the year of first publication and the name of the writer. For example "Copyright © 1994 Joe Writer." However, in WFH contracts, the copyright will belong to the company hiring you, which no doubt will put the copyright notice on all copies.

Find a good lawyer to look over all of your contracts, especially for a creator-owned property—don't be in such a rush for a job that you fail to read the fine print.

TOM MASON,
Co-founder, MainBrain Productions

COMPUTER ON-LINE COPYRIGHT LAW

In the last few years, computer on-line services have become much more prevalent and popular. Comics bulletin boards have opened up everywhere, and as a result, many newcomers have begun to post their writings for review, critique, and exposure. This brings up many concerns about legal protection and reproduction of the work. Here is a short piece excerpted from a longer article by writer Rob Wood.

All messages that contain original expressions of ideas, whether posted to [a computer] forum, sent privately [via e-mail], or uploaded to [a computer archive] library, are automatically copyrighted, as in any other "tangible medium of original expression." The Berne Convention, of which the U.S. is a signatory, did away with the need for copyright registration or even any mention of the copyright status on or in the piece itself. However, a copyright must be registered before a suit can be brought for infringement. Although the registration process can be instituted after the infringement takes place, certain rights will be lost in the process, such as the right to sue for statutory damages and recovery of attorney's fees. The sections of the Copyright Reform Act of 1993, which would have allowed full rights to the injured party, failed in Congress.

There are no major cases pending in federal courts as to the "tangible media" status of electronic literature and, in fact, all written forms of expression are copyrighted from the moment they are recorded. Copyright protection extends even to personal correspondence via regular mail. The law makes no distinction between letters, e-mail correspondence, forum messages, books, magazine articles, or any other form of written expression.

Not all subject matter in a written piece, whether electronically generated or printed on paper, is copyrightable, for example. Ideas are not copyrightable, either—only the original expression of ideas in a tangible medium are protected by law.

There is one area of copyright law and electronic media which is currently embroiled in controversy, and that is the area of "fair use" and whether or not publishers have an automatic right to distribute an author's work electronically. Fair use definitions in the Copyright Law were developed before electronic transfer of information became widespread, and they need to be clarified in the law in terms of the present situation; however, Terri Southwick, attorney advisor to The Working Group on Intellectual Properties, stressed that "fair use" can only be determined on a case-by-case basis.

Until recent years, this notice was a legal requirement to record your copyright in the federal Copyright Office. It is no longer legally required, but it is still strongly recommended. Many people misunderstand the law of copyrights—they believe that if there is no copyright notice, the work is "public domain" and may be copied freely. That is not the law, and it is a good way to get sued! However, if you put copyright notices on all copies of your original work, then you reduce the risk of unauthorized copying.

TRADEMARKS

Unlike the copyright notice, you cannot use the federal trademark symbol (®), until you have been granted a federal trademark registration. This is a long, and sometimes expensive, process. However, (most commonly in the case of artwork) you can use the letters "TM" under any character or logo that you create but have not registered. "TM" notifies people that you are claiming a "common law" trademark in your characters or logo. You could conceivably claim a trademark for any character that has come to symbolize the origin of your goods or services (like *Superman* for DC Comics). If you do not plan to re-use the character, copyright protection is all that needs to apply.

LICENSING

In the comics industry the subject of licensing can be divided into two distinct areas: a writer's work on licensed material, and the licensing of stories produced by a writer.

When you work on licensed materials, it means you are hired—on a WFH basis—to produce material based on established characters. The publisher who hires you has purchased a license from another company to create original materials based on those characters. The license entitles them to hire under WFH agreements only. All materials produced become either the joint possession of the publisher and the license holder or, as often happens, the sole possession of the license holder. An example of this would be the case of the *Star Wars* material which is owned by Lucasfilm although it is produced by Dark Horse Comics and the creators they hire. Many newcomers would be delighted to have an opportunity to work with these firmly established—and very popular—characters. On the other hand, the financial gain is limited, and the control the writer can have over the use of his or her work is nonexistent. Consider these facts carefully before signing a WFH agreement for licensed material.

Licensing of materials produced by a writer is another matter altogether. This means, if you create a particular character or story line, then you can control the licensing of that material. You can sell licenses to various publishers and merchandisers, and you control what is produced, and make a substantial profit from those reproductions. An example is comics professional Matt Wagner and his creation *Grendel* which he both wrote and drew. Although first published by Comico, it has also been licensed for use by DC and Dark Horse Comics. Another example of licensing is Dave Stevens' character, *The Rocketeer,* which he also wrote and drew. For many years, Dave licensed out the use of his character but a few years ago he sold his film rights to Disney/Touchstone Pictures.

There is a distinct difference between the two forms of licensing. Make sure you are clear about which one is specified if licensing is included in one of your contract agreements.

Find out what you're getting paid for, upfront. Don't just dive into a job because you're desperate to break into comics.

MIKE BARON
Comics Writer

FINANCIAL CONSIDERATIONS

As important as legal issues are for a newcomer, the financial aspects of managing your career are equally important. A solid contract will do you little good if you are unable to keep track of your income, overhead, and payment of taxes. Your awareness of these issues will also indicate to your employer whether or not you are a valuable addition to their creative staff, and will influence the likelihood of acquiring more work in the future.

The cardinal rule of keeping good financial records is:

KEEP ALL YOUR RECEIPTS!!!!

Although seemingly a burdensome task, over time you will find it becomes quite automatic. Many of those ostensibly inconsequential receipts will add up to big deductions at tax time. As you're now a self-employed freelancer, there is no one withholding taxes from your paychecks. Plus, you will be paying additional self-employment taxes. Those receipts will begin to seem like little slips of gold. Never, never throw them away!

Here are some simple, but important steps to better manage your finances:

1. *Invoice for every piece of work you do, and keep a copy of that invoice for your records.* Regardless of whether a publisher provides you with invoices, make out your own—even if it's just a handwritten slip of paper (although a more professionally printed or typewritten form is recommended). It is important to have your own record of income that you can track. A lack of a paper trail makes it a lot harder to collect your pay.

2. *Document the dates you ship the work and when monies are due on a calendar.* Keep track of income you are expecting. This way nobody will ever get too far behind in paying you, and your own creditors won't have to wait to get paid!

Make sure you know how long you should wait for a paycheck, and never let that allotted time stretch on.

DAVID LLOYD
Artist/writer

3. *Set up a simple bookkeeping system.* Develop a system to record all of your pertinent receipts as they apply to your income tax. Keep a file folder, box, tray or some type of receptacle handy in your office or home. Each day when you come in, dump in your receipts. At the end of the month (or every couple of months) set aside time to organize those receipts and record them.

At the end of the year when tax time rolls around, you are going to be very happy to have completed the bulk of the work. This system also provides you with a means to track your monthly and annual expenditures on various items like shipping and supplies. This will enable you to better budget your income, and help you in pricing out your work at a reasonable rate.

4. *Open a separate savings account to use exclusively for tax monies.* At the end of each year, Uncle Sam will collect approximately 25 percent of your gross income in federal, state, and self-employment taxes. The actual total varies between states, and depends on how meticulous you are about tracking receipts and deductions. It also depends on how much money you're making. Suffice it to say though, that if you keep a designated tax fund account, and set aside 25 percent of every check that comes in— BEFORE ONE PENNY IS SPENT!—you will find yourself comfortably protected at the end of the year when you have to file your income tax return.

   Also, once you have established a profit-making year, you will be required to pay quarterly estimate tax payments (every three months) based on your estimated income for that year. Failure to make these payments will result in big, fat penalty payments to the IRS (automatically calculated and billed by the IRS). It's in your very best interest to discipline yourself and regularly set that money aside. A little piece of advice—don't expect that your publishers will pay you a few weeks early, or give you a nice little advance around tax time. They are well experienced in the last-minute scramble by freelancers to produce tax payment money, and don't look on the practice too kindly. Few things will jeopardize your professional standing faster.

5. *Maintain a checking account to make business payments.* Many young freelancers like to keep their money as "cash on hand." This may seem like a good idea at the time, but here are a few excellent reasons for maintaining some form of checking account:

   - It is impossible to open a business account or establish a credit record without some type of checking account already established. If you want an account with your local office-supply store, or Federal Express, it won't happen unless you can prove established business ties. This means a credit history, which means an active bank account. Open one and use it.

   - It will greatly simplify your ability to keep track of business payments. To keep an accurate record of business expenditures, it is useful to have the check stub or copy as a receipt. Since sometimes you may forget to collect the receipt, may not be given a receipt, or may receive an unintelligible receipt, the checking record will greatly improve your record-keeping abilities.

6. *Use your bookkeeping records to create a comprehensive budget.* Once you've laid out an easy-to-follow bookkeeping record you can use the information it provides to guide you in budgeting your income. Track the amounts you spend on professional services, supplies, and expenses, and you will be able to determine how your money is being spent and how to better manage it. This will also help prevent that last-minute panic at the end of a pay period as you wonder from where and when you can expect your next dollar.

Karen Berger, Executive Editor for DC Comics

Credits Include: Oversees the entire Vertigo imprint (six editors and a large variety of books), edits *Sandman* and *Sandman Mystery Theater* in addition to a few creator-owned projects. Edited *SwampThing*, *Hellblazer, Shade, Animal Man* among many other series.

Question: What tactics would you recommend to aspiring writers for acquiring more work once they've completed their first comics job?

The number of unsolicited submissions that I get weekly, just at Vertigo, is phenomenal, so getting your foot in the door and having something bought is a major accomplishment, considering how many people want to write comics. The hardest part is over. However, it's still difficult if you don't have a regular assignment to keep the high industry profile that you need to get more work. I think the best thing you can do, assuming that you've sold your work in the genre and to the audience you strive to write for, is speak with editors and determine what type of material they're looking to acquire. Just doing cold, unsolicited submissions right after getting your foot in the door might not be the best route to take. It's better to get some direction, ask around. Find out who is looking for new material, what they are specifically looking for, and let them know you have some ideas for their books. Really be persistent. Follow up. Make it as easy for the editor as possible. The onus is really on the newcomer. You've already accomplished a difficult step by acquiring that first job, so you should try to sell yourself as much as you can. Ultimately, executing fresh and original ideas is what's going to get you there.

As a writer you should also keep yourself tuned to your creativity. Make yourself open to influences outside of comics.

Conventions can also be helpful. It's always good to place a name with a face, especially once you've sold stuff. And especially if you haven't previously met the editor you've sold to. Then it's definitely worthwhile going. Plus, there are so many companies out there, many of whom you might not know unless you go to a convention like the San Diego Con. Also, a published tearsheet of your work is a very helpful way of getting out samples. It makes it a lot easier for an editor than trying to read a script or a few page summary.

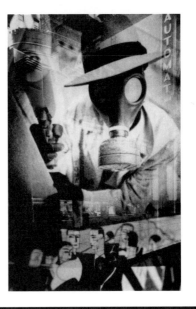

Art for Sandman Mystery Theater *by Gavin Wilson*

When you've determined where and how your money is being spent, you may find there is room in your income plan to designate savings for special circumstances, like travel expenses or financial emergencies (e.g., medical expenses, lost work and income, unexpected home or car repairs, etc.).

7. *Make a budget for convention travel and stick with it.* Since convention travel is a fairly critical part of being a comics freelancer, it's safe to say that you will most likely be attending at least one or two conventions each year. These little trips can be unduly expensive and if you don't take the time to plan a travel budget, you may find yourself tapping into next month's rent money!

Plan ahead for travel, accommodations, and meal costs, and then add at least 15 percent more. This method allows for a good travel budget, with a bit of leeway for unexpected situations that may arise. By planning your travel budget ahead of time, you will be able to set aside the money in smaller increments, which should help minimize the burden on your regular income and bills.

ORGANIZING YOUR FREELANCE BUSINESS

Good organization can be one of the most effective tools in successful business. It will make you a more effective—even powerful—businessperson. The most important areas a freelancer can organize include your office, work time, and travel schedule.

Office Organization

The physical organization of your work space is the most important aspect to focus on when honing your business organizational skills. By organizing your work space, you ensure that your work will be produced quickly, easily, and effortlessly—without the myriad distractions that can trip up the most earnest writer.

Make sure that your supplies and materials are conveniently stored. Keep more frequently used materials closer to hand. The less time you spend wandering around looking for the right paper, the pencil you want, a new typewriter ribbon, or a roll of fax paper, the more time you'll spend actually getting the work done.

If you ship your finished work to your publisher, remember to keep an adequate supply of shipping materials on hand: envelopes, boxes, cardboard, tape, shipping invoices, stamps, etc. If you are running on a tight deadline, you cannot afford to be delayed by the lack of appropriate shipping supplies. Keep a diligent check on your materials, and avoid last-minute emergencies because of unexpected shortages.

Remember to keep tabs on your other business supplies—the ones that enable you to conduct business: letterhead, business cards, sample sheets, etc. There will be many occasions where you might be put on the spot to hurriedly provide a potential employer with information. Don't get caught short and end up looking like a novice. Demonstrate your professionalism by being prepared. This advice also applies to your materials.

Organizing Your Files

One of the most important aspects of being a good, organized businessperson is maintaining effective records of your business dealings.

Good record keeping can protect both you and your employer's work interests. One of the first tasks you should set for yourself once you decide to pursue a freelance career is to set up a basic filing system. Take the time to organize your paperwork in a reasonable manner, without spending massive amounts of money on this endeavor, since inexpensive (or free!) cardboard boxes will serve adequately as filing cabinets. Do, however, invest a bit of money in a bulk package of file folders. Then, sit down and organize your paperwork in a manner that will work best for you. Create files for companies you deal with—your publishers—as well as general expense records—your business accounts.

By keeping up on your record keeping you will be able to better track your work, your income and business dealings with the various publishers. It will also help you keep tabs of your budget, supplies, and various business and financial responsibilities.

Scheduling Your Time

Organizing your work schedule efficiently is also a critical aspect of being a good businessperson. To be a successful freelancer, you need to learn how to estimate the time you will need to finish a project. If an editor offers you a regular series, assess the workload and determine whether you can meet the regular deadlines. If you are a newcomer who accepts a job and then fails to deliver on time, you will quickly find yourself hard pressed to drum up work. To put it more bluntly, you'll find yourself blackballed.

Some freelancers—both new and many of those who are firmly established—have an inordinate amount of trouble estimating the time that a job will take them. Sometimes this is due to inexperience. Sometimes it's due to plain old laziness. But often it's just due to poor organization.

Your first step toward improving your scheduling skills should be to get a calendar. Select one with a large, open, monthly grid where you can make notes about work deadlines, payment due dates, travel plans and any other pertinent business information. Get into the habit of keeping a written calendar record of every job you accept, and the date that it must be shipped to the editor.

When you send out a finished project and invoice for payment, make a note on your calendar of the date that money should arrive. Keep in mind that many companies have set dates for issuing payment checks, and allow for postal travel time. Keep tabs on those funds due, and follow up in a professional manner if they are late.

Find a good accountant to help you set up your tax planning so that you don't get hit each year with a huge tax bill from the government.

TOM MASON
Co-founder, MainBrain Productions

Also keep track of convention dates—both the major shows and any which you wish to attend. Regardless of whether you attend the larger conventions, making note of those dates will allow you to stay in touch with your editor more effectively, and eliminate those "limbo" days where they are at a convention and "incommunicado."

AN ORGANIZATIONAL STRATEGY:
Making Your Time Work for You Instead of Against You

Staying organized is the key to a well-balanced lifestyle, and doesn't apply to business practices alone. If your personal life is an unruly mess, chances are it tends to spill over into your business day. As a freelancer, disorganization can prove fatal to your career. A freelancer needs to set up a strict structure in which to work, since without a "boss" taking care of the day-to-day management problems can arise. Particularly when the freelancer works from home.

Many disorganized people don't think ahead when they are scheduling their day. And they don't have a realistic conception of time. They may estimate a task to take a certain amount of time—ten minutes, for example—when in fact it will take substantially more—say, two hours. These people need to learn to be more honest with themselves.

They also need to realize that you need to spend time to make time. In other words, spending some time to add organization to your life will, in the end, free up more time to relax or tackle those activities that are more meaningful. That is how you save time and that's how you can find time to do the things you love.

Here are some steps you can take to ensure you get the most out of your work time:

- *Just say no to time-consuming, tedious, high-stress work projects that will interfere with your regular working schedule.* This applies to both professional jobs (e.g., a favor to a friend who wants you to do some free work to help them out) or personal chores (e.g., agreeing to help your Mom organize her favorite fund-raising event). These jobs may seem acceptable at the time, but can ultimately drain you both financially and emotionally. Learn to set up boundaries and turn down work or chores that are unfulfilling, unnecessary, or harmful to your career. Also, learn to break monumental tasks into smaller chunks with more accessible goals.

- *Don't let day-to-day chores overcome your work time.* First, make a list of all the things that need to be done—both personal and professional. Then set time aside each day for working. Once this is done, decide how you will break up your daily work schedule for actual working time (writing) and general work chores (paying bills, returning calls, making copies, buying supplies, running errands). Divide those chores up over a workday, week, or month (depending on the size and frequency of the tasks). Give yourself rewards for completing blocks of chores. It will make your workday much more structured and efficient. This also works as an incentive for producing work when you experience difficulties.

- *Avoid distractions.* Most writers need truly uninterrupted time for producing quality work. This means no visitors, no phone calls, and no interruptions from family members. To make your work time more effective, designate a set time of the day—or specific day(s)—as your work time. Structure it to be uninterrupted time—except for emergencies—then lock yourself away and work. Designate your work area off-limits during those set hours. Make sure friends who tend to drop by unannounced are aware of your new schedule, and insist that they respect it. By structuring your schedule in this way, you will guarantee yourself some true writing time. If at first, or occasionally, you find you're having trouble producing, don't give up. Keep at it, writing anything at all. Train yourself to use that time to produce work, and soon enough you will do it effortlessly.

- *Budget your telephone time.* If you find that telephone calls (both business and personal) are taking a significant bite out of your work time, establish set telephone hours (this includes not taking business calls on weekends or during vacation time). Notify all your publishers of the hours during which you will be available, tell friends not to call during work time, and let your answering machine take the calls. If you can't afford a machine, unplug the phone or turn of the ringer. By letting yourself have uninterrupted work time, you will be able to produce more work, more effectively. Just remember to return the calls when you get your messages!

- *The three D's: Do It, Delegate It, or Dump It.* If you find yourself swamped with phone messages, mail, chores, etc., then use the three D's strategy. If you can do something within the next ten minutes, then do it. If you can have someone else take care of it for you, then delegate it. Otherwise, dump it for your attention later.

- *Keep a written To-Do list instead of trying to keep the chores listed in your head.* This way you can keep track of what you've accomplished and what still needs to be taken care of. Post-It notes are also a very useful tool, take up little space, and act as an excellent reminder. If you can't afford them, use scrap paper and tape or thumbtacks. By writing down your chores, you can keep better track of what responsibilities you have and how well you are managing them.

- *Periodically assess your current organizational strategy.* If you find you never have the amount of time you need to do your work and manage your business, then investigate new ways of mastering these problems. The more effective you are at your job, the more work will ultimately come your way.

Allow for convention travel time, as well as time to settle back into a work routine once you get home. Try to remember to allow for these trips, so that it will not interfere with your ability to deliver work. Few things can get you canned faster than if you attend a convention and your editor, or an associate of your editor, spots you there when you are already late on delivering work! If you keep track of your travel time, you will find it much easier to manage your work schedule and still fit in time to promote your current projects and line up new work at conventions.

Travel Organization

Another important area of organization is traveling to conventions. As simplistic as this may sound, for a freelancer this can be a particularly hectic and critical time.

The convention circuit is meant to help freelancers promote their projects, line up new work, and make business and social contacts. It generally entails taking at least a few days away from your work schedule (possibly more depending on how far way and how big a show it is). There are many things that must be done to properly prepare for a convention.

- **Making Travel Arrangements.** Because of the competitive nature of travel fees (e.g., airfare, car rentals, hotel rates) it's imperative that you make your plans far enough in advance to take advantage of the early booking discounts. Also, don't forget to mention the convention rate (which is usually a significant discount) when making hotel reservations, and to take advantage of any savings coupons (e.g., car rental/hotel packages). The money you save on travel expenses can be used to wine and dine a potential employer—or better yet, pay some bills at home! Planning ahead for travel dates will help you save money and the aggravation of getting last minute reservation in an over-booked city!

- **Make a Travel Checklist.** As over-organized as a travel checklist may seem, it's one of the most valuable tools I have developed since I started working as a professional freelancer.

  Early on in my career, I would scramble to gather clothing, toiletries, and my professional supplies at the last minute—sometimes only hours before leaving town. Without fail, I always left some crucial item at home and found myself sorely missing it or forking out big dollars in a strange city to replace it. Finally, in frustration, I sat down and made a comprehensive list of everything I would need for convention travel. I typed up the list and now keep it in a drawer with my travel supplies and, as a result, it's been a long time since I arrived at a convention unprepared.

If you take the time to plan your convention trips a bit more thoroughly you will find yourself a lot more relaxed once you arrive at the show. You will communicate professionalism, and potential employers can't help but see that.

COMMUNICATING EFFECTIVELY

The dictionary defines communication as ". . . the imparting or interchange of thoughts, opinions, or information by speech, writing, etc. . . ." Simply put, it means ask questions and be there to answer questions.

In the comics industry, this means that when you have a question for your publisher—regardless of the department involved—you call and get an answer. Don't procrastinate. Particularly if the answer will affect the finished product.

It also means that you need to answer your phone! Don't screen calls so you can avoid an irate editor who wants to know the whereabouts of his three-weeks-late book. Don't take the phone off the hook and claim you had calls all day just to avoid that same editor. If you don't already have call-waiting, get it. Or keep your social calls to a minimum during business hours.

As a freelancer in an industry that doesn't require you to live where your publisher is located, the onus is on you to be available to talk to your employer(s). Being available is the first rule of being a good businessperson.

Good communication has a lot to do with basic etiquette and general courtesy. Many people lack the basic communication skills necessary to be successful businesspeople. But that doesn't mean success will always be elusive. There are a plethora of books, courses, and therapy groups that can help you master the basic social skills needed for good communication—both listening and speaking.

If a lack of assertiveness is your problem, work on that. If nervousness interferes with your ability to converse easily, practice overcoming your inhibitions. These communication skills are mandatory. You will find yourself in a position where they are needed while at conventions, during interviews, in your letter-writing skills, and in basic telephone conversations. Nothing will more greatly jeopardize your chances at a job than your inability to communicate your needs and wants, as well as your abilities.

Telephone Etiquette

As I emphasized earlier, it is important to be available to answer questions, and don't hesitate to seek clarification when you have a question of your own. You need to listen carefully to what is said and answer appropriately. Try not to digress or behave in an inappropriately personal manner. Be polite, and remember, the editor you're talking to is probably swamped with work. They don't always have time to chat. Just because you sit at your desk or keyboard, wishing for a little digression from the work at hand, doesn't mean your employer has that same interest—or free time! Be considerate of the other person's time. Keep it simple, keep it clear, and keep it brief!

If you use an answering machine or voice mail, return the messages that are left. Your courtesy demonstrates your professionalism and can lead to future work.

The easiest way to infuriate a caller is with indifference. What a caller hates more than anything is people who are apathetic or act as if they don't care. Many editors are influenced in their hiring of a freelancer by the personality of the individual, and this includes phone style. You must learn how to communicate effectively, and in a friendly manner. When working with an editor, you must learn to be a sympathetic and attentive listener, find out just what the editor wants when he/she calls and what solutions or results he/she expects. This applies to your other business dealings and can also work for personal calls. Keep in mind that every time you converse on the phone in a

David Lloyd, Artist/Writer
Credits Include: *V For Vendetta* from DC Comics; *Night Raven: House of Cards* from Marvel Comics; *Philip Marlowe: The Pencil* for Byron Preiss; *James Bond: Shattered Helix* and *Hard Looks* for Dark Horse Comics; *The Horrorist* for DC's Vertigo Line.

Question: What tactics would you recommend to aspiring writers for acquiring more work once they've completed their first comics job?

For one, be as friendly as you possibly can to your editor.

Also, keep your eye on the trends, and what is popular in the published comics at that particular point. And make sure that you try writing every kind of story that is popular. Don't rely on one particular type of story that you especially like.

You should also check out the markets. Try and sell to every publisher in business, whether they are big or small, so that you explore every possible avenue.

Finally, use the weight of the small reputation you gain by selling that initial story as a good credential. There's nothing harder than trying to sell your stories if you have absolutely no other sales. Just making that first sale is so valuable. It indicates that you've been accepted, and are now working as a comics writer. You can use that as a tremendous tool to gain other employment. It often swings the balance. I think there are a lot of good writers who are struggling along, trying to sell very, very good work, but can't because they just haven't made that first sale. I don't think there are many editors who have enough faith in new writers to give them the breaks they deserve. So having been previously published-preferably by a major company rather than a smaller company—can be immensely useful.

Art from V for Vendetta

business call you are representing yourself as a business entity. Your phone manner can make or break a business relationship just by showing indifference.

It's also a good idea for any person in business to develop a pleasant phone personality. Most people don't think about how they come across on the phone. They don't stop to consider the tone of their voice or how the words they choose can put off a caller. It is also very helpful to "put a smile in your voice" when on the phone.

A friendly greeting and conversation will do much to improve your working relationships and will make you feel better, too.

Always remember, good phone etiquette isn't just good manners, it's an essential marketing tool.

Conventions and Interviews

You will have to meet and greet potential employers, fans, other professionals, peers, and sometimes even come face-to-face with editors you've only ever interacted with by mail or over the telephone. Communication skills are the basic building blocks of self-promotion. You can't hope to "sell" your skills as a freelancer if you are unable to communicate your abilities. This skill will help you "get your foot in the door," show your work, line up tryouts, make business contacts and even new friendships.

Letter Writing

This particular communication skill is required at all stages of freelance work, and as a writer is probably one of your most important tools. Unlike artists whose visual work is their primary sales tool, you must hook the editor and convince them of your writing skills with your letter. Before they even decide to look at your proposal or script, they will look at your letter. Be sure that your basic grammar, spelling, and command of English are good before you send out that letter. This can make or break your chances at being considered for a job.

You will need these skills when you first start out in your inquiry letter. You must communicate concisely what it is that you are interested in (acquiring submissions guidelines, work, etc.) and how you intend to go about getting it. You will also need these skills when you send in your samples (describing your abilities, your interests, and your work situation), and once you get the job, both in contract negotiations and execution, and in correspondence with your editor.

If you are unsure how to proceed with a business letter for any of these situations, invest in a book on letter writing or utilize the reference books available at your local library. Ask a friend, parent, or teacher who you are confident has the skill or knowledge to look over your letters or make suggestions on how to proceed. Just remember, keep it clear, keep it simple.

BUSINESS RESPONSIBILITIES

Demonstrating business responsibility is an equally critical aspect of being a good business-person. It means staying on top of your responsibilities as a career professional. And efficient and responsible handling of these jobs will ensure continued freelance employment.

Meeting Deadlines

You absolutely must be conscientious in making sure you meet your deadlines. When a publisher hires you to produce work, he or she is operating under a range of very strict deadlines—marketing, solicitation, production, printing, shipping, and so on. To have a successful and popular product means making all these deadlines on time. Therefore it is ABSOLUTELY CRITICAL that you deliver the completed work in the time frame you have

WRITER'S PORTFOLIO REVIEW PROGRAMMING

Writer's Portfolio Review programming was added to the list of events at a variety of conventions in 1994. A pre-registration sign-up is necessary to participate in the panel. At the panel, aspiring writer attendees are matched with established industry writing and editing professionals on a one-on-one basis. The goal of this matchup is to review a submission prepared by the writer. The submissions for the program are required to follow an established guideline—generally, a one-page, double-spaced outline of a writing proposal, plus a one-page sample of the scripting for that proposal. The writing sample is then critiqued by the professional.

I have asked a few of our top industry professionals for their opinion of the Writer's Portfolio Review programming.

John Ostrander, Writer

It's both a good and bad idea. This kind of programming helps to emphasize the role of the comics writer, and I think that's a good thing. And the industry needs good writers more than anything, at this point.

On the other hand, learning how to do a proposal is good, but that's not what makes someone a writer. They also must be able to write. If they submit a proposal that goes somewhere, but they can't deliver the script, then they've done themselves absolutely no good whatsoever. Additionally, it would be much more effective if the professionals were given the writing samples to review prior to attending the convention.

What I would prefer to see, and what I think actually works better, is a series of writing seminars at conventions. I don't mean writer's panels. I mean a single writer standing up there, teaching the basics. I think that a potential writer can learn more from a seminar, from somebody who knows what he or she is talking about and who is used to teaching, than can be learned in other types of programming. It would be more effective for a writer to have his or her work assessed in connection with a couple of days of this type of seminar program. But I think the whole seminar program has to be well-organized. And you have to organize the participants, so they can get some value out of professionals reviewing their work.

I could even see individual interviews between established writers and newcomers working effectively. Where the participant doesn't necessarily show his or her work, but instead has the opportunity to prepare several key questions that he or she would like to have answered by the professional. The interviews could last about 20 minutes with a given pro. This could also increase the accessibility of professional writers to convention participants.

I would even be willing to help in the organization if one of the bigger conventions were willing to implement these kinds of programs.

Roland Mann, Writer/Former Editor for Malibu Comics

I think these writer portfolio review programs are very beneficial to the industry, especially at the much bigger conventions. I think it is helpful to have a chance to have someone look at your submission. It's tough to sit down and look over someone's sample and say, "Oh, this is going to be a great story." However, what a professional can do is sit down and go over format with the newcomer and explain why nobody will read the proposal as it stands, and give recommendations like, "make this shorter," or "this is unnecessary here." It would be great to have a chance to go over ways the newcomer can "punch up" a writing sample. Even a one paragraph nutshell can have problems. A writer's portfolio review gives professionals a chance to show new writers how to better "sell" their work, and teach them how to develop a hook. With a sample page of scripting we can go through it and help the writer with panel descriptions, and go over what is expected or required by an editor. Giving new writers some critique on the actual mechanics of submissions is a great idea.

Len Strazewski, Writer

I think a writer's portfolio review session is a great idea. I like it. It's very difficult for a writer who does not have any kind of professional track record to demonstrate writing skills to an editor in an effective manner. This is true even at a convention when many editors are there specifically looking for talent. In order to demonstrate that you can write comics, you pretty much have to have your stories executed graphically—they have to be drawn. And that means that the art is always going to get the editor's attention first. Of course, if you're a newcomer it's unlikely that you have access to professional artists. You may be working with a friend who's an artist or who is also trying to break into the industry. That can magnify whatever weaknesses both of you have.

I think this kind of programming can work extremely well, but it takes editors or reviewers who are committed to examining the work, who are not just doing it because it's part of their "booth duty." These committed editors should sit down in advance and identify to themselves what they want out of a writer. Because too often editors will look at writing and not have a clear image of what they think demonstrates talent. Usually they look at it and say something like, "I don't know if this is any good, but if it is good I'll know it when I see it." When you're looking at the work of a new writer breaking in, you can't look at whether or not this story has fallen fully-formed, like a rock out of the writer's forehead, or if the writer is currently as good as Frank Miller or Alan Moore. You have to look at whether the newcomer has an ear for dialogue, and does he or she create story ideas that have motion, plot and activity? You have to look for aspects of talent that you as an editor, with your guidance, can pull together to make a fully fledged writer. I think it might be good to have some pretraining for the editor about how to review writers in this sort of unusual setting. Rather than preparing the writers, I would focus on getting the editors ready to look for the kinds of qualities that will make a good, professional writer.

Diana Schutz, Editor-in-Chief for Dark Horse Comics

This is a very good idea, but because conventions are so distracting and very high-stimulus environments, it's probably better if the editor/reviewer receives the writing sample ahead of time so that he or she has some time to look it over and digest it, rather than being forced to give an on-the-spot assessment and critique.

John Moore, Writer

I think it's really, really difficult to examine a piece of writing that's incomplete. You can examine a story idea to see if it's clear and well-stated, but there really isn't a way to say to somebody, "this is good," or "this is bad." I think it's limiting. A writer's workshop where writers could turn in a full script or the story for a full script would probably be more beneficial. It's just too difficult to take a single page of dialogue or a single page of script and judge the merits of the work based on that alone.

Giving the complete work to the critiquing panel ahead of time might work, but I think that to be of any real value it would need to be a more thorough workshop. Otherwise, I think it would probably be just as beneficial for an individual writer to hold a seminar where he simply tells the participants how he works in more of a step-by-step manner. Since different writers work in different ways, and the format actually differs depending on the dynamic of the creative team, having a writer teach a seminar can be very helpful. Some writers work very closely with their artists, some writers do full scripts and basically divest themselves of the script once it's done and have nothing to do with it afterward. In terms of format there's no one single correct form accepted by the industry, as there is in television or film.

I can't say that a writer's portfolio review for this short a time span would prove particularly beneficial for the would-be writer, but it might work if a group of professionals agreed to look at a set amount of work prior to the convention. But it would require a more complete script—either for a 10-page comics story or, more realistically, a full 24-page comic book story. An hour critique with each professional would be reasonable and helpful for the newcomers. Having material ahead of time is vitally important for the pros involved, because you just can't digest the work in the distracting environment of a convention.

agreed to. Publishing is rife with deadlines, and a successful freelancer needs to learn how to budget time to be a good and respected businessperson.

If you can improve your ability to reliably deliver consistently good work, there is a good chance that you will find yourself a well-respected creator in constant demand.

Proper Handling of Paperwork

There are many areas of our business that require filling out forms—contract agreements, invoicing, correspondence, rough drafts, shipping bills, checks, etc. It is imperative that you make a practice of completing the appropriate paperwork in a timely manner. Failure to do so not only affects your appearance of professionalism, but can also result in late payment for work and even worse, violation of work agreements.

As I mentioned earlier, the legal aspects of the business can make or break a professional career. If you take the time to responsibly review (that means READ CAREFULLY) your contracts, ensure that all appropriate signatures are thereon, and keep copies of all your contracts, you will be well protected in your business. Failure to do these simple things can result in gross violations on the part of less reputable publishers, to which you will have no response or recourse.

Keep careful track of your paperwork trail, and you will always have a clear record of your business dealings. Your publisher will be happy, you will be happy, and you can get down to the business of creating entertainment.

KEEPING YOUR HAT IN THE RING

Even after securing that first paying industry job, a freelancer must continue to actively pursue new work. The comics industry is a transitory business. Projects, publishers and freelancers come and go before you can blink twice, and what seems like a sure thing can be snatched away from you without warning. You may find yourself out of work and lacking income.

With this fact in mind, you should make a point of keeping your hat in the ring. Stay apprised of the sales of your project, be aware of the status of your publisher or the line they're using to market the work. Keep feelers out in the market to ensure that you have a selection of backup jobs in the wings. You may also want to take on the odd single piece or small one-shot job (scheduling permitting, or course) just to make sure that your name remains highly visible in the market.

Follow the same steps you took when looking for work, to make your availability known:

- Send out updated samples and proposals regularly.

- Occasionally call around to "shoot the breeze" with new business acquaintances (other freelancers, editors, publishers, convention organizers, retailers). This will give you an opportunity to renew your friendly ties, pick up any news, and keep your name on their minds.

- Make sure you take full advantage of conventions. This is an excellent place to continue forging social and business relationships, and a fertile source for obtaining

Len Strazewski, Writer

Credits Include: Co-creator of Ultraverse's *Prime* (with Gerard Jones) and *Prototype* (with Tom Mason), one of the seven founding Ultraverse writers, *Elven* mini-series from Malibu Comics; *Justice Society of America, Starman, The Flash, The Fly* and *The Web* (Impact Line) from DC Comics; *Speed Racer* and *Die Kamikaze* from Now Comics; *Trollords* (editor and creative consultant) from Tru Studios, Comico and Apple Comics; *Hero Cycle,* a "creative landscape" for use in all aspects of marketing.

Question: Once a newcomer gets work, what business behaviors do you believe are critical to being a successful professional?

Probably the single most important thing is to be on time. It's very important to show a publisher that you can perform within the parameters that they establish. The key thing to getting repeat work is getting your work in on time. This means meeting deadlines.

It also means being careful with your creative input, to stay within their continuity, and in general being responsive to their publishing parameters. They're going to have goals that they want you to meet in terms of story, timing, and the way you interact. You have to be able to maintain a very professional relationship. Sometimes that's not necessarily easy. Sometimes it means having to sit on the phone and listen to an editor tell you what you already know, or getting an earful of stuff that you just really don't want to do. But you still have to be responsive to

new work. Psychologically, you will be more in demand as a freelancer if you're already working. Editors will wonder what they're missing, and you'll find yourself with plenty of work offers and suggestions.

- Court other projects and editors within the company you work for. If you enjoy your work relationship with a particular publisher, there's nothing wrong with doing the majority of your work with that company. Ask your editor or others in the company about upcoming projects for which they might consider you.

- Don't hesitate to approach other related markets. The comics industry has ties and associations with many other markets that would be interested in your freelance skills: games, books, magazines, movies, television, etc. Don't restrict yourself to the comics industry if you have other interests. Many of these related industries can provide lucrative sources of income. In addition, they give you a second audience that can be drawn over to follow your comics work. Take advantage of any markets that will help promote you as a talent.

that. It doesn't mean that you need to prefab a story from them, or that you just take dictation. But it does mean that you have to be responsive to them. You have to show them that you're listening, and that you understand their ideas. And as much as possible, you try to accommodate their ideas and needs within the context of the story.

In particular, helping an editor when they're in a jam is important. Most of the writers who work regularly in comics got their start because an editor needed a fill-in story, or needed something done on an emergency basis, and called up and said, "Look, I really need a story. Can you do this for me?" When you're just getting started, your answer has to be pretty much, "Well, of course I can!" And then do it. Then eventually you'll get

Art from Terror Tots

into a regular schedule. Being the person who can help an editor in a stressful time is one of the best selling points a writer has.

Pay your taxes. I know folks who haven't, and as a result they've gotten themselves into a lot of trouble.

LOUISE SIMONSON,
Writer

Stay Apprised of What Is Happening in the Industry

It is important to be informed if you hope to be a successful businessperson. You need to follow the trends and fads that are drawing the readership, and how your work will fit into the market.

There are a number of news publications that report regularly on happenings in the industry. These include *The Comics Buyer's Guide* (weekly newspaper format), *Combo Magazine* and *Wizard* (monthly color magazines), *Comic Scene* (monthly newsstand color magazine), *Comic Shop News* (weekly color news flyer) and *The Comics Journal* (monthly black-and-white interview magazine). The distributor catalogues also provide a valuable source of information about what's available in the market. Read one or more of these publications regularly and you will find it much easier to stay on top of where you fit into the comics industry.

Remember to update your business files using information you acquire in your reading and convention socializing. This will pay off both in terms of acquiring new work and in carrying on an informed and intelligent conversation with new business contacts.

Self-Promotion

As a freelance writer you might believe that it is solely the responsibility of the publisher to promote your work, since it is their product. Well, to a certain extent that's true. However, you should also be aware of two things: your future work can depend on how often your name is in the public eye, and most publishers are producing so much product that they can't possibly afford as big an advertising budget as you would hope or expect. So, what do you do to solve this dilemma? It's simple: you do some self-promotion.

Self-promotion means taking the reins—at least to some degree—and helping your publisher promote your project. Self-promotion can be done in many ways, and the time and expense you devote to it can pay off for you both financially and in terms of more work. Increased sales of your work due to a higher profile will bring you bigger royalties. Your publisher will be impressed and will appreciate that you have taken such a serious interest in the success of your work, so they will want you on board for other jobs. Additionally, other publishers will see your work more often, with good sales, and will also want to hire you.

What exactly can you do to self-promote? Well, the answers are endless, but to make it a bit simpler and more direct, here are three basic steps you can personally take to ensure your work gets good exposure.

1. Send out press releases to industry publications and major newspapers every time you have a big project about to ship, or sign onto a name project. Although many publishers will send out press releases, most publications like press releases that provide the basic information plus quotes from the principal(s)—that's you! Write your own press releases, to ensure that the information is correct. Make sure it's okay with the editor—and if so, maybe get a quote from them, too. Create a set mailing list for the releases, and send them out regularly. Try to use strong, exciting letterhead or press release forms provided by many computer word-processing applications, to catch their attention. And keep an eye on the publications for when your news is published. Clip and save the info and, as a courtesy, send copies to your editor or publisher for their files.

2. When your newest work is released, and provided that you have sufficient complimentary copies, send a press copy to a select group of industry publications. Make sure you have a specific (and receptive) individual targeted for this copy, and hopefully your work will get a (kind) review. The exposure will be great for sales, and the trade folks will appreciate you thinking of them. Plus, everyone likes to get free stuff—they're no exception!

3. Make sure you attend conventions when you have a new project just released, or imminently due for release. Your presence at these cons will give you the opportunity to talk up the project and—if you make or get access to them—to hand out excerpts from the project. Most fans and editors are interested in what's new and what's coming out. Plus, your excitement will be contagious, and they will look for the work when it's released. Remember, there's so much comics stuff out there that if they don't hear about it, they won't know to buy it!

There are an infinite number of methods of self-promotion, and various good books out there to guide you through those waters (see Appendix C). If you truly want to succeed, you must be willing to invest time and energy in the business of your craft. The combination of producing quality work and self-promotion will make you a recognizable industry force.

ADVANCES IN TECHNOLOGY AND HOW THEY AFFECT YOU

The state of the comics industry has been profoundly affected by technological advances over the past decade. Most recently, the use of computers and facsimile machines has become more than commonplace—it is an accepted, expected form of working. For you, the freelancer, this means you must become much more informed, aware and skilled with these technologies.

Facsimile Machines

For those in the know, the fax machine (as it is more commonly called) is one of the most indispensable—and now very accessible—tools of the decade for comics. Very few competent business people operate without one. With the rising costs of shipping and postal services, the fax machine has provided an easy, inexpensive and immediate way for editors and freelancers to communicate.

Additionally, fax machines have come down to an affordable price level in recent years, and any dedicated career professional would be very wise to set aside savings earmarked specifically for acquiring one. Not only will it ease your workload by cutting time on replies, it will save you money on shipping materials and costs. It will also demonstrate to your editor that you are serious about your writing career in comics, and that you are a true professional.

If for some reason a fax machine is just not financially feasible at the moment, there are a couple of alternatives. One is to look into a nearby fax service. Many office-supply stores, shipping services, copy shops, and small businesses offer fax services for a minimal cost. Get the number, and offer it to any business contacts interested in your fax information.

Another solution for sending faxes is to use someone else's machine and your telephone credit card. With your card you can use any fax machine to send a document without creating expense for the owner of the fax machine. Simply feed in your original document, dial the target phone number, enter your telephone card number, and transmission begins. The charges will appear on your monthly telephone bill just like any other long-distance call.

Then, when your finances permit, invest in a machine of your own. It also will help as a tax deduction!

Kurt Busiek, Writer

Credits Include: *Green Lantern, World's Finest, Justice League of America, Legend of Wonder Woman* and *Valor* for DC Comics; *Liberty Project* for Eclipse; *Vampirella* for Harris; *Johnny Demon* for Dark Horse Comics; *Spectacular Spider-Man, Web of Spider-Man, Darkman, Power Man/Iron Fist, Marvels* for Marvel Comics; *Teenagents* for Topps; *Youngblood Strikefile, Regulators, Velocity* for Image.

Question: What value to do you think computer on-line services can have for aspiring comics writers?

I'd have to say it's a mixed bag. The big pluses of computer on-line services are that they're like a 24-hour, 365-days-a-year convention. You get to "talk" to publishers, editors, writers, artists, letterers, colorists, retailers, and a broad variety of readers, from eager mainstream fans to the snootiest of the elitists. It's an interesting mix, and I can't help but think that anyone interested in comics will find something of value in the experience.

But at the same time, the aspiring writer is going to find himself up against a lot of the same obstacles that he or she would be in any other circumstance. Professional writers are going to be just as wary of reading sample plots or scripts and giving feedback on them, for fear of being accused of plagiarism in the future. Editors are going to be just as harried and have just as little time to review submissions (less, probably, since the time they spend on surfing the net cuts into submission-reading time). So there probably isn't a huge chance that the aspiring writer will find people willing to give him feedback, instruction and support—except for his fellow fans, of course. And that's a good option right there—a lot of the fans you'll find on the net are articulate, knowledgeable people who may deliver better creative feedback than an aspiring writer could expect to get from a pressed-for-time editor or writer, anyway.

Also, the benefit an aspiring writer should be looking for isn't limited to creative feedback. Participating on the net and "listening" to what working professionals (whether they're on the publishing end or the retail end) have to say, will give the

Many publishers are amenable to receiving written copy via modem or e-mail. If you have access to a computer and an Internet connection, you can save considerable time and paper by using this electronic medium that has become an accepted part of the business transactions in the publishing industry. Just be sure to find out in advance if this form of submission is acceptable to your publisher, and ensure that you have the correct e-mail information. This is a terrific alternative to a fax machine.

would-be pro a much better idea of how the industry operates—and that's something he needs to learn at the same time as he's honing his craft. It's a good place to keep abreast of the latest news and rumors—if a new line has just been started up, or if an editor has just had a book canceled (creating an opportunity for writers to pitch new ideas)—it's liable to turn up on the Internet well before it gets to the industry press, since the net doesn't have to wait for typesetting, printing and shipping. [Of course, the flip side to that is that the people who post news on the Internet haven't necessarily checked their facts, so a snippet of rumor on the computer may well turn out to be false. You get the news first—but you have to separate the good stuff from the garbage on your own.] This expediency isn't specifically of benefit to an aspiring writer—it'll help a would-be penciller for the same reasons—but it's good information to have at your fingertips.

Of course, the social aspects of the on-line services play a part, too. When I was breaking in as a writer, I know of at least one opportunity I got because I had a lot of fan letters published, and the editor in question knew my name and thought I'd offered intelligent, well-expressed comments. So he figured I stood a decent chance of delivering intelligent, well-crafted stories too, and gave me a shot. If I hadn't written all those letters, he wouldn't have had any reason to give me a break. The Internet is an updated, immediate version of that sort of thing—a would-be writer who posts their comments on the Internet may impress editors by being articulate and thoughtful, and so when that writer's submissions come in, the editor may be more likely to give them more than a cursory reading. [And as always, there's a corollary to that—if a would-be writer is rude and obnoxious on the Internet, the editor may be aware of that, too, and reject his submissions out of hand, simply because he's decided that the guy's a jerk. But how you behave on-line is up to you...]

All in all, I'd say there is plenty of good to be gotten. Be careful, though—the single biggest drawback of being on-line is that it's addictive, and you may find yourself having such a good time conversing with others on the net that you don't get any work done. And all the input in the world won't help you if you don't actually do the writing you're trying to sell.

Computer Technology

Although not everyone can afford to purchase a computer, if you are one of the fortunate folks who has one, a whole new world will open for you as a writer. If you suffer from some degree of anxiety about the new computer technologies, then start small. Read some material on computers and how they work so you can learn the limits and possibilities they represent. Start out with some easy software, a game, or simple program.

Familiarize yourself with this before graduating onto the more complex software. By using your computer in small steps, and then becoming more familiar with its abilities, you will find yourself taking slow but steady strides into this exciting and efficient field.

On the personal computer end of the business, you have access to good word-processing software that can make your writing and formatting effortless. Additionally, there are excellent spell-checkers and thesaurus programs available to add polish and proofing to your work. There are even grammar-checkers available for those less sure—or more careful—about their work. A computer can also offer you an excellent way of creating your own letterhead and business cards, and help you handle your bookkeeping, taxes, and contracts. With CD-ROM capabilities, it also puts massive reference volumes at your fingertips with a minimum of space consumption.

Computer on-line services open yet another world for you as a writer in the comics industry. Whether you choose a general-service Internet provider (ISP) CompuServe, or America Online (just to name a few), you will have access to a vast array of reference sources and public libraries, as well as comic publisher web sites. Additionally, most on-line services offer bulletin boards or forums, and include areas especially for comics. These forums offer library information, contact with other newcomers, and on-line access with many established, name professionals—both freelancers and publishers. Taking advantage of on-line services can help you stay on top of the status of the industry, news, and grapevine information about new projects as they come up. It also provides you with an opportunity to forge social ties that may ultimately benefit you on the work front further down the road.

SELF-IMPROVEMENT

As a freelancer, you must make a concerted effort to continually improve your writing skills. Only in this way will you guarantee a continual flow of writing jobs. Learning new self-promotion techniques for use at conventions, improving your skills at making social contacts or networking, and keeping industry contacts apprised of your current work status are all ways to improve yourself professionally.

Most business people have untapped talents and smarts just waiting to bloom. To follow are a few suggestions to help your writing career in comics take off.

- Make the most of your work situation, no matter how frustrating or limiting it may seem. Just because it isn't the top-of-the-field glamour job writing for *X-Men* or *Batman,* doesn't mean that you shouldn't do your best work. Even if things seem bad, always remember the Chinese character for "danger" also means "opportunity."

- If you seem to be lacking in financial or economic acumen, then check out a few business books or publications. Money and capital influence everything in our work and personal lives—from taxes, to retirement benefits, to buying groceries. By learning a bit more about financial influences on your career, you may be better able to influence how your earnings grow.

- Cross-training is more than a fad. Don't hesitate to learn new skills in your work; it will make you more valuable to the publisher and you'll be less likely to need to hunt for work. Just because you prefer to write a regular series, doesn't mean that an occasional back-up, one-shot, or annual won't be a good thing for you to try. If your strengths are currently in plotting long, intricate stories, try taking a shot at short, short fiction—say an eight-page back-up, or prose for the back of a trading card. The more skilled you are at your job, the more in demand you'll be.

- Enroll in classes. Any kind of education that will help you improve your work skills—whether it's writing expertise or confidence building training—makes you a more effective business person.

- Learn stretching and relaxation exercises to keep yourself loose. Repetitive-stress injuries flare up when tension builds up in your body and mind. In a job that tends to be as sedentary as writing, these techniques can improve both your attitude and productivity, and help you prevent having chronic problem such as back pain or headaches.

- Seek advice from more experienced colleagues—or from a new or younger colleague with fresh ideas. Sometimes just opening a dialogue will give you a whole new perspective on your work and approach. Plus a professional support system is both helpful and gratifying.

- Learn creativity techniques to break out of stale, old patterns of thought. For writers, this is a critical skill since the potential for succumbing to a "writer's block" is always present. Find ways to break those old patterns, and give your mind a "stretch."

- Think about the entire scope of your career. Be sure that this is the kind of work you truly want to do, and are prepared to pursue aggressively. Consider reading career-changing and job-seeking manuals that help outline ways to assess your career choices. Be sure that the work you're currently doing is the kind of comics work you want to do—don't get pigeonholed into superheroes if you want to write straight action.

- Since it's likely you've never been an editor, cut them some slack. Remember, it's a tough job and not everyone has all the skills necessary to do it perfectly. The more consideration and courtesy you show your editor, the more likely he or she will return that respect.

- Learn about the management concepts of teamwork and consensus-building. Although these concepts apply to the corporate world, comics is a teamwork industry. We work with other creators, editors, publishers, distributors, retailers, and convention organizers. By mastering these teamwork skills, you improve these relationships, and your cooperative abilities will ultimately lead you to more work and stronger professional ties.

- Learn about employment laws that apply specifically to freelancers and the publishing industry. By being informed about your freelancer rights and responsibilities, you will be more confident in your business dealings. And that confidence will be easily perceived by an employer.

Bill Messner-Loebs, Writer/artist

Credits Include: *Journey* from Fantagraphics; *Johnny Quest* from Comico; *Wonder Woman, Hawkman* from DC Comics; *Sanctuary: A Life on Street Level.*

Question: Do you believe that hiring an agent or a lawyer is beneficial for writers? Would you recommend this practice to newcomers?

When I was trying to break in as a professional science-fiction writer, I remember specifically going to a seminar where Lloyd Biggle, the science-fiction author was asked that question. He said, "Generally, you can only get worthwhile agents once you no longer need them." But several of the other people at that same seminar said, "But for God's sake, don't get one for your first book, because the only people who you can get are going to rip you off!"

In comics, there are rights and so forth that you may not know about, and if you have a very good agent, they might be able to get you a better contract— especially on less well-known projects. I don't have an agent, and my few attempts at acquiring one have never worked out very well.

Right now there's a new phenomenon called an "agent/packager." It's pretty hard for even established writers to just show a script to an editor—even one they have a relationship with—and get a response. If you don't have a big-name artist talent to illustrate your writing, having an agent who is a packager and who can line you up with an artist, might be useful.

I would say that a lawyer would be beneficial for a comics writer, but with the proviso that we're talking about for a professional who already has regular work. I would say that a lawyer is not necessarily recommended for newcomers. Don't weigh yourself down with a lot of ancillary personnel before you actually have an income that you need to protect. To that end, I would echo Maggie Thompson [editor of *The Comics Buyer's Guide*] by saying that what's more important than either an attorney or an agent, is an accountant. However, it's important to have a relationship with an attorney available to you. But a lawyer

• Share your business expertise, knowledge or skills with a charitable organization. In addition to the altruistic rewards, there are benefits to both your community and your social contacts. Charitable events are supported both at the community level and, through conventions, at the national level. There is a vast array of comics industry-supported charities. Investigate ways to get involved.

• If you're interested in expanding your publishing horizons on a global level, study a

Art from Messner-Loeb's Journey

won't do you much good on your work-for-hire assignments with the mainstream companies, since they have their set contracts.

They're not really going to listen to you [contractually] unless you've got a lot of clout. You can't say "Oh, I'm sorry. I won't write Batman for you unless I can own him!" That is unlikely to happen.

However, you will be sent contracts, and it's nice to have somebody you can run them by. You should probably ask around to your more experienced peers about a good comics/entertainment lawyer. While regular lawyers can be helpful (and have been helpful to me in the past) on bizarre contracts, for the most part they don't really understand what a small business comics is, and may advise you a bit too conservatively. One of my favorite comments I've heard has been, "This is a dangerous, dangerous contract!"

But it's always better to talk to an attorney than not, and a decent one is not going to be that expensive for the first hour.

new culture or language. Comics are published worldwide and are translated into a multitude of languages. By incorporating various cultures and belief systems into your work, and being familiar with those cultural systems, you broaden your audience and make your work richer and more textured. Additionally, if you are offered the opportunity to travel to another country to promote your work, you will be better prepared!

Joe R. Lansdale, Writer

Credits Include: *Jonah Hex: Two Gun Mojo*, *Jonah Hex: Riders of the Worm*, *Blood and Shadows* (artist, Mark Nelson) from DC Comics; *The Lone Ranger: It Crawls* from Topps Comics; *Tarzan's Lost Adventure* from Dark Horse Comics; *Mucho Mojo* (novel), *Two Bear Mambo* (novel), *Savage Season* (novel), *Cold in July* (novel) from Mysterious Press; *Writer of the Purple Rage* (short story collection) from CD Publications; *Batman: Captured by the Engines* from Warner Books.

Question: Do you believe that professional associations like Science Fiction and Fantasy Writers Association, Horror Writers Association, and the Comic Book Association Professionals are beneficial to aspiring comics writers?

Art by Mark Nelson for Blood and Shadows *from DC Comics*

Perhaps, to a minor degree, they're beneficial to beginning writers. I don't think they do you much good once you've broken in. In fact, I've pretty much separated myself from all organizations. Not out of any meanness or spite, but because I don't see that they do anything for me. Also, the things I can do for other writers I can do just as easily without belonging to the organizations.

I'm almost of the opinion that what they do for aspiring writers is also very limited. The only thing they seem to do is give people a connection with other folks who are doing what they are doing—in this case, writing. Which when you first start out is hard to find. Once you've met all these people and get connected with them through that sort of organization, then I think it has really served its purpose. But some people are really worked up about the awards given by the associations. It's always nice to be considered and to win an award based on the choices made by your peers, but on the other hand I don't feel that awards have influenced, helped, or hindered my career in any way. And I've won a bunch of them. So I don't know that organizations make that big of a difference.

Sometimes they can also be helpful for providing a market list of available publishers. I speak more as a writer of prose here—I don't know much about the comic book organizations, since I don't belong to any of them.

- Try different communication styles. Master negotiation skills and create a dialogue in a way that benefits everyone; you don't always have to win a discussion or debate. If you talk too much in your professional situations (something to which I can sheepishly claim to be somewhat expert), learn to listen more. If you don't talk enough, speak up more.

- Start saving and investing for your retirement. Traditional pension plans are disappearing, and there's not much chance that social security will be around when you need it. It's never too early to begin saving for retirement. Who knows? You might want to retire young!

Become a freelancer who is flexible, multi-talented, inquisitive, and entrepreneurial. It'll help you thrive in the industry and it'll do wonders for your personal happiness.

APPENDIX A

GLOSSARY OF TERMS

alternative work: Comic content that does not tend to follow the established and acceptable superhero format.

anthology: A collection of stories in a single volume. Usually done by more than one writer/artist team. Many companies use an anthology for three reasons: (1) to showcase smaller or alternative projects by their established creators; (2) to introduce new characters and stories that may be spun-off into their own series; and (3) to offer a venue for newcomers to try their hand at comics.

appearance: A public appearance by an established comic professional. Usually at comic stores or conventions. The professional will sign autographs, talk with fans, sell his or her work, and, in the case of artists, do original sketches.

banner-head: The company name or logo for a specific line or category of titles, i.e., Vertigo, is the banner-head for DC Comics' alternative comic book line.

bill of sale: A form stipulating to the buyer of an original work just what rights, if any, they are purchasing with the work.

billing invoice: Similar to a payment invoice, although generally provided by the creator to bill the employer.

comic script: The written manuscript that details the plot, action, descriptions, and dialogue for a comic book or story.

computer on-line services: Computer service available, via modem, through telephone lines, that links the user with a communications and data base. Often provides bulletin boards and forums for specific topics and areas of interest in addition to a variety of specialized services.

contract: A written instrument that outlines the agreement between creator and employer. Can take a multitude of forms, including work-for-hire and creator-owned rights.

convention or con: An event held by a local sponsor over one or more days, which features a display of industry-related material by retailers and publishers, guest creators, panel discussions, and exhibits.

convention circuit: The regular, and often annual, schedule of conventions. In the comic industry, the majority of conventions are held during the spring and summer.

copyright: Stipulates who holds ownership of a work for reproduction purposes.

cover letter: The single-page correspondence sent with a sample package to an editor. The cover letter serves to introduce the freelancer to the editor, by providing information about education, past work experience, and skills. It also outlines the type of work in which he or she is interested.

creator: A freelance writer or artist.

creator-owned rights contract: A contract in which the creator maintains most, or all, of the reproduction rights for the work produced for an employer. Most common contract form with the smaller, independent creator-supportive companies.

creator rights: The right to control the reproduction or publication of a character/concept created by a professional. The publisher's degree of control can vary and should be outlined in the contract. These rights are relinquished in all standard work-for-hire agreements.

critique: A structured or relatively formal situation when you obtain opinions and comments on your work from industry professionals, including other creators, publishers, and editors. Also an assessment by an individual (can be another creator, editor, publisher, or fan) of the caliber and quality of your work. It should include comments about technical expertise, individual style and expression, dynamic qualities of the work, presentation, and overall impression. Comments should be used to improve upon the work, and future work should be tailored to publisher requirements.

cross-over series: A comic series in which characters from different books—and sometimes from different companies—interact in a single issue or series.

distributor catalogues: Also called order books or solicitations.

editor: The publisher employee who oversees the creation and production of a comic book. They are assigned, or may choose, the variety of projects they oversee to completion. They are expected to be the quality-control person and primary communication path in the comics-publishing chain. They are generally over-worked.

feedback: An informal critique of your work samples provided by an editor or professional. This advice can be invaluable in the continued improvement of your skills. You also receive feedback during a more formal critique.

full-style script: A script laid out as if the action were to occur on film or stage. Descriptions can include panel by panel or page by page descriptions. Characters are described in detail, and all dialogue, captions, and sound effects are included.

generated collectible: A limited comic industry item (book, trading card, toy, print, etc.) that has become a collectible because of high demand. For example, if only 1,000 copies of a book are printed, but the advertising and promotion generates 7,000 interested customers, then that item becomes a collectible. Publishers that produce intentionally small editions of guaranteed hot-selling items are generating a collectible.

genre: A class or category of artistic endeavor having a particular form, content or technique, i.e., super-hero vs. horror vs. science fiction, or it can mean inked vs. painted, depending on the context of use.

graphic novel: Generally considered to be a 48-page comic book with a square-bound cover, although many other book lengths and formats have also been considered graphic novels.

header (page): The information that runs across the top of every page of a script. Should include title of the work, name of author, and the script page number.

indicia: A block of publishing and copyright information that appears in fine print inside published matter. In comics often found on the bottom portion of the inside cover, front, back, or title page.

letter of intent: An outline of the elements of a contract agreement in letter form.

licensing: A formal agreement between the author of a work and an individual or company that wishes to reproduce that particular work.

margins: The white space or border surrounding an area of text on a single page.

mini-series: A self-contained story "arc" for a specific character(s). Generally spans between two and six issues.

"Name": An established or fan-favorite comics professional whose name can help enhance product sales.

negotiation: Discussion between a creator and employer about the pertinent items to be covered by a contract.

networking or "schmoozing": The popular name for the act of making business introductions and connections with potential employers during social activities. Often can involve a friendlier, less-businesslike approach.

Number 10 envelope: A legal-size, white envelope. Dimensions are $4\frac{1}{8}''$ x $9''$.

outline: The "bare bones" version of the story: a brief description of the plot, subplot, action, and character interaction. Generally used to propose a story to a potential publisher. All key characters are described, their relationships to and with each other, and the ways and means by which the action proceeds.

page rate: The price per page paid to a creator for their work. May be paid between 10 and 30 days after publisher's receipt of work. Generally paid when the work is completed.

panel discussion: Generally held during a convention, it features a panel of "authorities" on the topic of discussion. Topics range widely, and the panel duration can run anywhere from 30 minutes to an hour or more. There is often a question and answer period for the audience.

payment invoice/chit: A form that is filled out and signed by the creator, billing employer for work done. Often provided by the employer, but also can be provided by the creator. It can also include a contract agreement in the fine print.

permission to reproduce work in publication: A simplified contract form that focuses on the right to reproduce the work.

plot: Everything that happens in a story. It is built of significant events with important consequences that comprise the story. A plot is the idea developed into a story.

plot-style script: A script in which the action, individual pages, or comic book as a whole are described in outline form. Once the artistic team produces roughed-in art, with each page designed and action laid out, the writer adds dialogue and captions.

point-of-purchase: The place from which a comics industry product is purchased by the general public (i.e., a comic book store counter).

publisher: The individual in charge of all aspects of the complete product line for a company. May also be the owner of the company and/or an editor.

purchase order: A printed form from an employer requesting the completion of a particular work, which can sometimes act as a contract.

quarterly estimates: Tax payments made four times a year based on income earned in the preceding year. These payments are required by the IRS from self-employed income earners and they help to defray the impact of the end-of-year tax payment.

reading: Established or new writers read excerpts of their written work to an audience of peers and/or the public.

reprint: Republication of an already published comic story. May be reprinted in the same format as another edition (First, Second, etc.) or may be reprinted in another format (graphic novel, trade paperback, anthology).

reprint rights: The rights that can be bought and sold to reproduce a work for publication, merchandising or licensing.

response card: A quick and easy alternative to the self-addressed, stamped envelope. Preprinted with stock responses that an editor can check off, this card can help supplement your mail-out log information. It also saves on postage costs if formatted as a postcard.

retailers: The owners and operators of your local comics store. They are responsible for ordering the books that are purchased by the readers. Their orders determine which books sell well, and frequently shape the editorial choices of the publishers. At a convention they are also called "dealers."

rights and permissions: An area of publishing that handles the reproduction of a company's property by both businesses and nonprofit organizations.

royalties: A percentage of the profits after all production expenses have been paid, including company expenses and page rate (generally considered an advance against royalties to come). Expressed in percentage form and based on numbers of books sold. For comics, the royalty is usually divided between creators who work on a book.

sample: A sample of written work, which should include a plot or outline, and a page of sample scripting. Generally used to interest a publisher in employing you as a professional.

SASE: A self-addressed, stamped envelope (usually a #10, legal size) provided with a sample submission to facilitate a response and/or return of samples by the editor. It should accompany every mail submission you send to a publisher.

script: The fully written text of a comic book story laid out in such a manner as to describe the story elements—plot, character, and action—and to tell the story from beginning to end, detailing both the art and the written aspects of the story.

script format: The manner in which a script is formatted. Includes the margins, titles, page headers, spacing, and capitalization.

scripting style: The style in which the script is written. The two most recognized styles are Plot-style or Full-style scripting. Additionally, many comic writers have created their own style of scripting that is a combination of these two styles. Most comic publishers are very flexible on the style of scripting accepted and used by the company.

self-publishing: Acting as your own publisher for producing a comic of your own creation. A popular and viable alternative to selling your creations to another publisher.

share of profits: A portion of the total profits from publication of a book, after production costs have been paid. Generally expressed as a percentage and in place of an advance page rate.

slush pile: A stack of unsolicited submissions received by a publisher. Generally quite large and not consistently scrutinized. It is difficult to acquire comics work if your scripts end up in the slush pile.

small press: Publishers that produce a small number of titles and a small number of issues of each title. Also called "independents," they include many self-publishers. Successful small press companies include Caliber Press and Dark Horse Comics.

solicitation: Copy used to "advertise" a new book from a publisher. Usually found in a distributor catalogue or a publisher flyer.

sound effects: The text of a script that details sounds occurring in the comic story. For example a phone ringing could read; PHONE: **Brrrring!**

spec, "on spec": An abbreviation for speculation or on speculation. Sometimes jobs are obtained based on the "speculation" of the publisher, meaning that they take on a project or creator hoping it will be profitable in the future.

standard forms: Preprinted or typeset forms that can be used as a type of contract. They can take the form of a letter of intent, bill of sale, permission for reproduction form, or a billing invoice.

submissions guidelines: Written rules provided by publishers to act as a guide for new talent

submissions of artwork or writing. These guidelines stipulate the form and method for unsolicited material. Aspiring pros should strictly adhere to these guidelines for serious consideration of their work.

taxes: A crucial part of the business end of being a freelancer, self-employed taxes and social security taxes are required in addition to federal income tax. Freelancers are frequently required to make quarterly estimated payments to the IRS.

tearsheets: Copies of published work that can be used as samples.

thumbnail: A small, rough sketch showing the image to appear in a panel or on a page in a comic book.

title (script): The block of text appearing at the top of the first page of a script that identifies the name of the work and the author's name and contact information. It can also include the date, total page count for the comic story, a brief description of the contents (e.g. a three-issue mini-series), and any copyright notice.

trade paperback: Can be either the paperback version of a hardbound book, or a compilation of two or more books of a series into a single volume.

unsolicited submissions/material: Mail submissions sent to a publisher without their invitation, with the hope of being considered for future work.

vanity press: A small press business that usually publishes work for a fee—this means that the creator pays them, they do not pay the creator.

video/film-style script: A script laid out as if the action were to occur on film or stage. Descriptions can include action descriptions (panel by panel) or scene descriptions (page by page). All characters are described in detail, plus all dialogue, captions, and sound effects are included.

work-for-hire contract: A contract in which reproductions of the work produced becomes the sole property of the employer. It is the most common contract form with major comic publishers and on licensed characters (such as movie characters).

BUSINESS FORM SAMPLES

Joe Scriber - Scripts and Stories
123 Writers Way,
Booktown, PA 77577
(123) 456-7890

BILLING INVOICE

To: _____
_____
_____

Date Due: _____ Invoice Number: _____ Date: _____

Quantity	Description	Price

SS#: 123-45-6789 **TOTAL** |_____|

Sample of a freelancer invoice

DARK HORSE WORK VOUCHER

PLEASE PRINT LEGIBLY   ☐ CHECK THIS BOX IF THIS IS THE FIRST TIME
YOU HAVE EVER INVOICED DARK HORSE

NAME: _____ DATE SENT: _____

ADDRESS: _____

_____ ☐ CHECK HERE IF THIS IS A NEW ADDRESS

PHONE #: _____

SOCIAL SECURITY #: _____

BOOK TITLE: _____ ISSUE #: _____

JOB #: _____

REVISION 072392   KEEP THE GOLD COPY FOR YOUR RECORDS. RETURN THE OTHER COPIES WITH YOUR WORK.

TYPE OF WORK: _____
DATE DUE: _____
PAGE RATE: _____
NUMBER OF PAGES: _____
TOTAL DUE: _____

DATE ACCEPTED   EDITOR'S AUTHORIZATION
_____   _____

Sample of a company invoice

FUNNY PAGES PUBLISHING
CONTRACT AGREEMENT FORM

This agreement is entered into between Funny Pages Publishing (hereinafter "Publisher") having a publishing address of 1234 Big Time Avenue, Urbania, NY 10101, and Joe Scriber (hereinafter "Writer") having an address of 123 Writers Way, Booktown, PA 77577.

The effective date of this agreement shall be March 01, 1999, for the comic book feature "Super Musclemen in Tights."

The "work" as used herein shall mean a fully executed script for six 24-page issues.

Writer is hereby employed by Publisher to do the work. Publisher shall have the exclusive right to reproduce the work for any and all other purposes, and the work shall be considered a WORK-MADE-FOR-HIRE. Publisher shall have the right to direct the development of the work and determine final acceptability of the work. If work is determined unacceptable, Writer will be given the opportunity to make appropriate changes within a reasonable time period as agreed upon by Writer and Publisher. Publication of the work signifies acceptability.

Writer agrees that the work shall be completed in a timely fashion, as agreed upon by Writer and Publisher. Time allowed for the work to be completed has been set as one month per issue.

As compensation for the services to be rendered by Writer under this agreement, Publisher shall pay Writer as follows: $85.00 per page plus 1% royalty on wholesale price for sales over 50,000 copies.

Writer and Publisher hereby agree that Publisher shall make payment NO LESS THAN 30 DAYS AFTER APPROVAL OF WORK. If Writer has not been contacted within 48 hours of receipt of work, that work shall be deemed approved.

Publisher agrees to give a credit line for Writer in the published comic book feature. Publisher will send Writer 15 complimentary copies of the comic book feature, in which work by the Writer appears, once it has been published.

Funny Pages Publishing   Writer

_____   _____

By: Al Watcher, Chief Editor   By: Joe Scriber

Date: _____   Date: _____

Sample of a work-for-hire contract

FIERCELY INDEPENDENT BOOKS
CONTRACT AGREEMENT

This agreement is entered into between Fiercely Independent Books (hereinafter "Publisher") having a publishing address of 987 Small Press Road, Printer, Il 99789, and Joe Scriber (hereinafter "Writer") having an address of 123 Writers Way, Booktown, PA 77577.

Effective March 01, 1999, the Publisher agrees to employ the Writer to produce a 32-page, one-shot graphic novel entitled "Sherlock's Sister" (hereinafter "Work").

The Publisher agrees to pay the Writer a $500.00 flat fee advance against royalties of 7% of wholesale, after printing expenses, as compensation for First Printing Rights of the Work. Payment will be made within 30 days of receipt of the finished Work. If the Publisher does not pay the full amount within 30 days of receipt of Work, a late charge of $20.00 per day will be added to the cost of the work, up to a maximum late charge of $500.00. Execution of the Work will begin upon verbal and/or written approval from the Publisher, and will be delivered no later than June 01, 1999, provided that approval is given no later than May 15, 1999. If Work is not delivered by this date, a late charge of $20.00 per day will be deducted from the cost of the work, up to a maximum of $500.00 in late charges.

In the event that the Publisher decides not to use the finished Work, they will be required to pay the Writer a "kill fee" payment of $200.00.

The finished Work is copyrighted by Joe Scriber, and the Publisher is entitled to First Printing Rights only, for the 32-page one-shot graphic novel entitled *Sherlock's Sister*. All other rights will be negotiated separately.

The Publisher will provide the Writer with 25 complimentary copies of the published Work.

Fiercely Independent Books   Writer

_____   _____

By: Joan Witness   By: Joe Scriber

Date: _____   Date: _____

Sample of a creator-owned rights contract

APPENDIX C

RESOURCES

READING LIST

Reference Books

Following is a selected list of reference books, available to writers. These encompass both the business and legal aspects of your career, as well as how to create and improve your work. Take the time to check out at least one or two of these publications. Many are available in your local library or can be ordered through your local bookstore. These books are invaluable tools to conduct business with some authority. I have noted with an asterisk (*) the publications I have found most useful as a professional.

*Buchman, Dian Dincin & Groves, Seli. *The Writer's Digest Guide to Manuscript Formats*. Cincinnati, Ohio: Writer's Digest Books, 1987.

Caputo, Tony. *How to Self-Publish Your Own Comic Book*. New York: Watson-Guptill Publications, 1997.

*Crawford, Tad. *Business & Legal Forms for Authors & Self-Publishers*. New York: Allworth Press, 1990.

Crawford, Tad. *The Writer's Legal Guide*. New York: Hawthorn/Dutton, 1996.

Davidson, Marion and Blue, Martha. *Making It Legal: A Law Primer for the Craftsmaker, Visual Artist and Writer*. New York: McGraw-Hill, 1988.

Eisner, Will. *Comics and Sequential Art*. Florida: Poorhouse Press, available exclusively from Kitchen Sink Press, Inc., 1985.

David Emblidge and Barbara Zheutlin. *Writer's Resource*. New York: Watson-Guptill Publications, 1997.

Field, Syd. *Screenplay: The Foundations of Screenwriting*. New York: Dell Books, 1998.

*Garvey, Mark, Ed. *Writer's Market*. Cincinnati, Ohio: Writer's Digest Books.
(Note: This is an annually updated publication, and the title is generally preceded by the year.)

Holm, Kirsten C., Ed. *Guide to Literary Agents & Art/ Photo Reps*. Cincinnati, Ohio: Writer's Digest Books.
(Note: This is an annually updated publication, and the title is generally preceded by the year.)

*Kremer, John. *1001 Ways to Market Your Books*. Iowa: Open Horizons, 1993.

McCloud, Scott. *Understanding Comics: The Invisible Art*. Massachusetts: Kitchen Sink Press, Inc., 1994.

Schultz, Dodi, Ed. *Tools of the Writer's Trade*. New York: HarperCollins Publishers, 1990.

Straczynski, Michael J. *The Complete Book of Scriptwriting*. Cincinnati, Ohio: Writer's Digest Books, 1996.

Trade Publications

Below is an alphabetical list of a few of the important trade publications for the comic industry. As a professional it is in your best interest to stay apprised of the status of our industry. These publications can help provide you with the information you need to be an informed freelancer. Check out one or more of these regularly.

The Aspiring Cartoonist
P.O. Box 18679
Indianapolis, Indiana 46218

Combo Magazine
990 Grove Street
Evanston, Illinois 60210
(847) 491-6440

The Comics Buyer's Guide
700 E. State Street
Iola, Wisconsin 54990-0001
http://www.krause.com/collectibles/html/bg.html

Comic Scene
475 Park Avenue South
New York, New York 10016

Comic Shop News
1266 W. Paces Ferry Road #445
Atlanta, Georgia 30327
(404) 261-8181
http://www.dreamsville.com/CSN/

The Comics Journal
7563 Lake City Way
Seattle, Washington 98155
http://www.tcj.com

indyWorld Magazine
611 NW 34th Drive
Gainesville, Florida 32607-2429
(352) 373-6336
http://www.indyworld.com

Wizard Magazine
151 Wells Avenue
Congress, New York 10920-2064
http://www.wizardworld.com

SCHOOLS

There are a variety of good schools that offer writing training, but only a few offer some degree of writing instruction applicable to the comic book industry. You can look into these programs if you would like to refine your writing skills, or check out your local community college or university extension, which are excellent sources of educational opportunities for those who can only participate in part-time course work. Writing courses offer a big plus: They force you to write and they force you to submit what you write to the scrutiny of others. If you want to be a pro you must learn how to present your work and accept critical feedback.

As a writer, there are a wider variety of options available to you for improving your skills than for comic artists. Many writing classes provide excellent training even though they do not specifically focus on comics writing. Schools that offer film classes can also be valuable since many screenplay-writing classes provide training that is highly applicable to comics. Check out listings in your local telephone book to see what is available in your area.

Here is a listing of a couple of educational institutes that offer writing classes tailored for comics, and some of their requirements. Write for complete details and an admissions package.

The Joe Kubert School of Cartooning
37 Myrtle Avenue, Dover, New Jersey 07801
(201) 361-1327
Tuition (subject to change): For 1998 - $7,700.00, not including room and board.
Requirements:

- High school diploma or equivalent degree.
- Complete and mail application form with non-refundable $25.00 fee.
- Respond to two essay questions.

The School of Visual Arts
209 E. 23rd Street, New York, New York 10010
(212) 592-2100
Tuition costs are available by mail inquiry only.
Requirements:

- High school transcript.
- 250-word essay on reason for wanting to attend the school, including goals and interests.
- Personal interview if you live within 250 miles of New York City.
- Complete application form with non-refundable $25.00 application fee.

Correspondence Courses

The Writer's Digest School
P.O. Box 12291, Cincinnati, Ohio 45212-0291
(800) 759-0963
Tuition costs vary depending on writing course selected and payment plan chosen.
Requirements:

- Complete an application.
- Complete course within two-year period.

SOFTWARE FOR WRITERS

With the advent of computer technology and advances on the Internet, there are now a vast array of programs available to writers, and many that will benefit writers interested in pursuing a career in comics. Here is a selection of programs specifically targeting script writing and story development that may be of interest to you. Formatting software will conform your material to professional screenplay standards, and story development programs will assist you in creating the material.

Formatting Software

Final Draft (Windows 3.1/95 or Mac 3.5)

- flexible, easy-to-use.

- built-in word processor.

- uses fast function-key macros to create elements needed for a professional screenplay.

- automatically inserts "More" and "Continued" at top and bottom of page breaks.

- includes spell checker, thesaurus.

- lists at approx. $229.

PlayWrite ScreenWriter (Mac)

- designed just for submission screenplays rather than full production scripts.

- includes many of the functions found in Final Draft and Scriptware.

- built-in word processor.

- uses an Icon Bar for single-key access of style elements.

- incorporates nearly 100 programmable macros for customized formats.

- lists at approx. $149.

ScriptThing (Windows, MS-DOS)

- created by a working writer and former script coordinator.

- handles formatting and page breaks automatically on screen and in real-time.

- fully automatic (More)s and (Cont'd)s, Top and Bottom Scene Continueds, Act/Scene numbering.

- intelligent text recognition.

- huge range of automation from its most basic two-key inputting to SmartTab and QuickType.

- fully automatic numbering handles all the A and B scenes and pages.

- tracks all revisions and omissions during writing and editing.

- single keystroke generation of full production breakdowns.

- lists at approx. $285 for Windows, $199 for DOS (production version), $149 for DOS (freelance version).

Scriptor (Mac, MS-DOS)

- add-on to Word and WordPerfect.

- includes Vocabulate, which analyzes the vocabulary of the script, based on word frequency, uniqueness, and more. Helps to track voice consistency in character's dialogue.

- will also produce a detailed report on the script.

- lists at approx. $150.

Scriptware (Windows, MS-DOS)

- one of the most flexible formatting programs available.

- built-in word processor.

- formats screenplays, treatments, outlines, and letters.

- can import text files from other programs.

- also available with just the film and TV essentials as Scriptware Lite ($129).

- lists at approx. $299 for Windows or Macintosh and $179 for DOS.

Scriptwriting Tools (add-on for Microsoft Word MAC)

- conforms scripts, writes treatments, and creates storyboards.

- uses 10 style templates that include standard script formats, two treatments, storyboards, and questions lists.

- lists at approx. $80.

StoryCraft (Windows, MS-DOS)

- story-processing program—designed specifically for writing screenplays and novels.

- designed by WGA-member and former Screenwrite Now!-columnist John Jarvis and the noted wordsmith Irwin Berent.

- creates full novels and screenplays.

- aids in fully developing the story premise and developing the story concept. Will identify your script by Category (Action or Theme) and Type (from 14 basic types). Will detail main character, their helpers, and their worlds. Match the story you want to write with the precise set of time-proven Structure Steps adapted from the classic works of fiction.

- incorporates the ideas of leading literary teachers, past and present developing the plot twists within each Structure Step.
- uses all major word-processing editing features. Will allow you to print out your work at any point and skip quickly to any stage of your story. Will also allow you to import and revamp previously created stories.
- lists at approx. $79.

SuperScript Pro (add-on for WordPerfect MS-DOS)

- configures scripts for feature films, screenplays, TV dramas, sitcoms, and stage plays.
- paginates any existing WordPerfect document.
- automatic scene numbering and page flow.
- "More" and "Continued" at end and beginning of pages.
- lists at approx. $99.

Writing Screenplays (add-on for Microsoft Word for Mac or WordPerfect MS-DOS)

- incorporates essential functions found in more sophisticated software while utilizing the power and features of a separate word processor.
- lists at approx. $40.

Story Development Software

Collaborator (Mac, MS-DOS)

- based on the classic three-act structure of drama.
- uses Aristotle's six elements of drama.
- challenges you to develop and enhance your story and characters through a series of questions.
- lists at approx. $199.

Dramatica (Windows 3.1/95, Mac)

- designed to aid in the creative building of developed characters, character interaction, plot structure, and theme.
- lists at approx. $399 for Pro version and $149 for Writer's Dream Kit version.

Plots Unlimited (Mac, MS-DOS)

- helps to brainstorm ideas for stories and plots.
- uses a database of more than 5,600 conflict situations, which provide the structure for developing a plot outline.
- can be a valuable springboard for new ideas.
- lists at approx. $299.

StoryLine (Windows 3.1/95, Mac, MS-DOS)

- interactive program that challenges you to create and polish the elements that make a good story using a 22-step approach to story structure.
- easily exported into a word-processing program.
- lists at approx. $295.

WriteWare CD Application Bundle (Windows and Mac)

- exclusive collection of over 35 different shareware, freeware, demo-software programs, and electronic books for screenwriters. Contains programs ready to assist in developing concepts, fleshing out characters, outlining plots, and writing scripts in correct screenplay format as well as five electronic books and coupons for selected software programs, screenwriting products, and services.
- formats your screenplays.
- develops your plots and characters.
- lists at approx. $19.95.

Internet Locations for Scriptwriting Software Information:

Reviews from the Writer's Guild of America:
http://www.wga.org/journal/1996/0796/scriptware/intro.html

Internet Filmmaker's FAQ
http://www.iffrotterdam.nl/if-faq/if-faq3.htm

Screenwriter's FAQ
http://www.panam.edu/scrnwrit/chap14.html

Software for Scripts
http://www.teleport.com/~cdeemer/splayrev.html

CONVENTIONS

Here is a listing of the more established comic conventions and trade shows in North America. I have tried to include conventions representing major geographical areas (i.e., Northwest, East, South, Midwest). This list includes the approximate month that the convention takes place and the contact information where you can get additional data about the particular convention is also included. Conventions with an (*) are highly recommended for newcomers trying to get exposure with publishers.

Alternative Press Expo
Time: February
Location: San Jose, California
Alternative Press Expo
311 Fourth Avenue #512
San Diego, California 92101

The Big Apple Comic Convention
Time: November and January
Location: New York City
The Big Apple Comic Convention
67-53 Woodhaven Boulevard #102
Rego Park, New York 11374
http://www.digdomdes.com/bigapple/

*Comic-Con International/San Diego Comic-Con
Time: July or August
Location: San Diego, California
Comic-Con International/San Diego Comic-Con
311 Fourth Avenue #512
San Diego, California 92101
http://www2.comic-con.org/comicon/

Dragon Con/Atlanta Comics Expo
Time: September
Location: Atlanta, Georgia
Atlanta Comics Expo/Dragon Con
P.O. Box 47696
Atlanta, Georgia 30362-0696
(770) 623-6321
http://www.dragoncon.org/

Heroes Con
Time: June
Location: Charlotte, North Carolina
Heroes Con
P.O. Box 9181
Charlotte, North Carolina 28299-9181
(704) 375-7464

Mid Ohio Con
Time: November
Location: Columbus, Ohio
R.A.P. Productions
P.O. Box 3831
Mansfield, Ohio 44907
http://www.wfcomics.com/midohiocon/
Attn: Roger Price

Motor City Comic Con
Time: May
Location: Novi, Michigan
Time: October
Location: Dearborn, Michigan
Motor City Comic Con
19785 W. 12 Mile Road Suite 231
Southfield, Michigan 48076
Attn: Michael Goldman

Small Press Expo
Time: September
Location: Bethesda, Maryland
Chris Oarr
P.O. Box 5874
Takoma Park, Maryland 20913
(301) 565-8340
http://www.indyworld.com/spx/

Wizard World formerly (Chicago Comicon)
Time: July
Location: Rosemont, Illinois
Wizard World
c/o Wizard Magazine
151 Wells Avenue
Congress, New York 10920-2064

WonderCon
Time: April
Location: Oakland, California
WonderCon
1001 Broadway
Oakland, California 94072
(510) 464-1120
http://www.wondercon.com/

World Convention
Time: April
Location: Toronto, Ontario
World Convention
341 4th Street
Midland, Ontario
L4R 3V1 Canada
Attn: Maggie Hamilton
(705) 526-6699

PROFESSIONAL ASSOCIATIONS
There are a number of professional associations connected with comics and peripheral to comics that are worth learning more about. Membership in

one or more of the organizations can provide you with a wealth of advantages. In addition to legal information and a structure for getting professional support, many of these associations also offer emergency assistance, group health insurance, and legal assistance. Most importantly, they offer you a network of professional peers from whom you can gain both social and professional contacts.

Here are a few of the key professional associations and their contact information.

Comic Book Legal Defense Fund
Founded in 1986, it operates as a watchdog organization to protect comics shops and creators from prosecution that threatens First Amendment rights.
PO Box 693
Northampton, Massachusetts 01061
(800) 99-CBLDF
Fax: (413) 582-9046
E-Mail: cbldf@compuserve.com
http://www.cbldf.org

Comic Book Professionals Association
Founded in 1992. Operates as a comics professionals-only organization. Striving to arrange airfare discounts and group health insurance, among other benefits, for freelancers.
P.O. Box 570850
Tarzana, California 91357-0850
Contact: Noel Wolfman, Executive Director

Comic Art Professional Society (CAPS)
Professional society for comic artists and creators. Requires members to have already achieved professional status. Meetings are the second Tuesday of each month.
P.O. Box 1440
Burbank, California 91507
Contact: Pat McGreal, President

HWA—Horror Writers of America
Professional association for horror writers. Provides a range of services, benefits and information, in addition to a contact system for peers.
5336 Reef Way
Oxnard, California 93035
Contact: Virginia Aalko, Executive Secretary

SFWA—Science Fiction and Fantasy Writers of America
Professional association for science fiction and fantasy writers. Provides a range of services, benefits, and information, in addition to a contact system for peers.

5 Winding Brook Drive #1B
Guilderland, New York 12084
Contact: Peter Dennis Pautz, Executive Secretary

Words and Pictures Museum
A professional-caliber museum, associated with numerous universities and art institutes, featuring comic book art and writing. Established by Teenage Mutant Ninja Turtles co-creator, Kevin Eastman.
140 Main Street
Northampton, Massachusetts 01060
(413) 586-8545
http://www.wordsandpictures.org

COMICS PUBLISHERS
Here is a partial listing of some of the better-known comic book publishers. If you wish to send in a submission, contact the company using a SASE, and request a copy of their submission guidelines from their submissions editor. Keep this listing as a reference in your business files.

Internet Listing of Comic Book Publishers
http://www.indyworld.com/comics/industry.html

Acclaim Comics
275 Seventh Avenue, 14th Floor
New York, New York 10001
(212) 366-4900

Antarctic Press
7272 Wurzbach, #201
San Antonio, Texas 78210
(210) 614-0396
Attn: Herb Mallette
http://www.antarctic-press.com/submissi.htm

Archie Comic Publications
325 Fayette Avenue
Mamaroneck, New York 10543
(914) 381-5155
Submissions Editor: Victor Gorelick

Caliber Comics
225 N. Sheldon Road
Plymouth, Michigan 48170
(313) 451-9830
http://www.calibercomics.com/basicsub.htm

DC Comics, Inc.
1325 Avenue of the Americas
New York, New York 10019
(212) 636-5400
http://www.dccomics.com/submit.html

Dark Horse Comics
10956 SE Main Street
Milwaukie, Oregon 97222
(503) 652-8815
Attn: Jamie Rich www.dhorse.com

Disney Comics
500 S. Buena Vista Street
Burbank, California 91521
(818) 567-5739

Fantagraphics Books
7563 Lake City Way
Seattle, Washington 98155
(206) 524-1967
http://www.fantagraphics.com/submission.html

Gladstone Publishing
P.O. Box 2079
Prescott, Arizona 86302
(602) 776-1300

Harris Publications
1115 Broadway, 8th Floor
New York, New York 10010
(212) 807-7100

Image Comics
1440 North Harbor Road, #305
Fullerton, California 92635
(714) 871-8802

Kitchen Sink Press
76 Pleasant Street
Northampton, Massachusetts 01027
(413) 586-9525
http://www.kitchensink.com

Marvel Comics
387 Park Avenue South
New York, New York 10016
(212) 696-0808

Sirius Entertainment Inc.
P.O. Box 128
Stanhope, New Jersey 07874
(201) 347-6611

Slave Labor Graphics
979 S. Bascom Avenue
San Jose, California 95128
(408) 971-8929

Topps Comics, Inc.
One Whitehall Street
New York, New York 10004
(212) 376-0300

Viz Communications
653 Bryant Street
San Francisco, California 94107
(415) 546-7073

COMICS DISTRIBUTORS

Under the auspices of the Independent Association of Direct Distributors (IADD) there are a number of large distribution companies with wide-ranging business locations. Here is a listing of some of the more noteworthy distributors.

Big Picture Distributing
1 Westside Drive, Unit 12
Etobicoke, Ontario, M9C 1B2
Canada
(416) 622-9196
Fax: (416) 622-5783.
E-Mail: news@bicpicture.on.ca
Distributes: Comics (worldwide)

Bud Plant
P.O. Box 1689
Grass Valley, California 95945
http://www.budplant.com

Cold Cut Distribution
1729 Angela Street, #2
San Jose, California 95125
(408) 293-3844
Fax: (408) 293-6645
E-Mail: comics@coldcut.com

Diamond Comic Distributors,
1966 Greenspring Drive, #300
Timonium, Maryland 21093
(800) 45-COMIC or (410) 560-7100

Downtown Distribution
1938 West County Road C
Roseville, Minnesota 55113
(800) 733-8529
Fax: (612) 898-4065
E-Mail: townmail@sprintmail.com

SyCo Distribution
13251 Occoquan Road, Suite 129
Woodbridge, Virginia 22191
(703) 492-8787
E-Mail: spears@kingroach.com

SUBMISSIONS GUIDELINES

Following are the writer's submissions guidelines from select companies (those who provided the information on request) in alphabetical order. These guidelines were current at press time and were provided by the publisher or submissions editor.

Use these as a strict guide when sending samples of your writing work to the company.

ACCLAIM COMICS

Include a self-addressed, stamped envelope. This allows us to respond in a timely fashion—within one to two months of receipt of your submission. Work will not be returned nor will a reply be given if a self-addressed, stamped envelope is not enclosed.

Please do not submit creator-owned properties. We are concentrating on our existing universe. At this time we are NOT looking for original work. Please submit material that pertains directly to the Valiant universe.

Direct your submissions to the attention of our Submissions Editor. We will look at only typed or printed material. Make sure what you submit is as professional as your intentions. Grammar and spelling errors distract the reader from the content of your work.

Do not send original work; photocopies are fine. Please make sure to put your name and address on every page.

Please don't telephone to monitor the progress of your submission. All work will be evaluated.

CALIBER PRESS

At Caliber Press, we try to keep everything as simple as possible, hence this brief letter about our guidelines.

First off, all of our books are strictly paid on a royalty basis after publication. No page rates, no guarantees, no advances. We have tried different methods and this is what works best for us and our creators. The amount earned is totally dependent on sales. If the book does really well, then the creators do. All of our books are in black and white. We have done color in the past but are very reluctant to do so now.

Creators maintain complete ownership of their material right from the beginning. We allow creators a great deal of control of the production aspects as well. Our motto is "it's your book" and we truly feel that way.

We don't put together teams on books. We don't match up writers with artists, pencilers with inkers, etc. Proposals should come in with the writer and artist set already. We help you with the lettering, but that too comes from the creator's royalties. We allow creators to do their own covers if they want (virtually all of them do and most do fully painted covers.) We don't have a great need for colorists or cover artists because of this.

What we want to see on a proposal is a rough idea of what the series will look like, where it's going, etc. Art-wise, we need to see at least a few pages of finished continuity so we can have a feel for what it looks like. Scripts should include some dialogue.

Please do not plan on doing a 38-issue epic. Most series will never get that far. Plan on one to six issues. If you want to continue after that, you can always do another mini-series or continue past the original story line.

The most important thing to realize is that when working in the independents, you're not likely to make a great deal of money. Some people can make a living from it, but most cannot. Over half of the over 400 comics that come out every month have sales of 3,000 or less. Be realistic in what you're expecting. The best way to approach it is to do the work for the love of it or think of it as a stepping stone to prove yourself, or to do a project that you really want to do regardless of sales. We're not trying to be overly pessimistic here, but comic work is hard and frustrating, so be prepared.

To follow is a brief description of the types of material that we are looking for. Please remember that we get hundreds of submissions a month, and that sometimes we can't answer them as fast as we would like. Especially during busy times of the year such as the convention season and major holidays, like Christmas.

We hope that this letter is taken as an honest approach and does not discourage you from submitting to us and other companies. Always make sure that you check out titles from the company that you are submitting to, so you are aware of what it is they do. Sometimes a proposal will be rejected because we're already doing something that is very similar. Other times, it is evident that the submitter has no idea about what the company he or she is submitting to does.

Be sure to enclose a SASE (self-addressed, stamped envelope) if you want a reply. If you want your work returned, send along an envelope large enough, with sufficient postage. If you do not send a SASE, more than likely you won't hear from anyone. After all, if you don't care about your work enough, why should we? Besides, the expense is enormous when added up over the course of a year, and all this for material we don't want to use!

Please don't call us a day or two after you have sent in your proposal. We probably haven't had a chance to look at it yet. We allot certain days for looking through submissions and sometimes our schedule just can't fit it in on a particular week. Do not send submissions Next Day or Federal Express. It's a needless waste of money.

The best way to show your stuff is to send letter-sized photocopies. NEVER SEND ORIGINALS!! Do not send scraps of paper that are not connected. If you're sending out a lot of proposals, the best thing to do is invest in a rubber stamp and stamp your name, address and phone number on every page.

What We're Interested in

This may sound flippant, but what we're looking for is material that is good, regardless of subject matter. We do a lot of material that is different from what's out there, but we also do some of the more conventional stuff as well. Caliber is a very diverse company that has done zombies, westerns, war, punk detectives, horror, science fiction, superheroes, slice of life. . . you name it. We've probably done just about every genre.

Things to generally stay away from, unless it's something that's really different and/or good; the science fiction epic, Dungeons and Dragons, westerns (after seven issues, we've just about given up), and funny animals. That's not to say that we won't do something in those areas, but it is much harder to come up with something that is different or unique.

Many of our titles are more sophisticated, yet not adult. Though hard to categorize, titles in this line include *Baker Street, Taken Under, Silencers, Warp-Walking, Fringe, Deadworld,* and *Realm.*

We also have a few anthologies that accept submissions. Again, these will be based on a pure royalty payment system. Most of the time we would prefer complete stand-alone stories, but we are willing to look at some serials if most of the work is complete.

Whatever route you choose, we wish you the best of luck!

DC COMICS

If you'd like to try writing for DC, we suggest that you send a query letter to the editor of each title you're interested in submitting your work to. You must include a self-addressed stamped envelope with sufficient postage or an international reply coupon or there's no guarantee you'll receive a reply.

Address submissions to the specific editor you are interested in contacting. Many of our editors (such as the Superman and Batman editors) are unwilling to read unsolicited submissions for their titles. Some editors will look at work from new writers.

If an editor is willing to look at your work, send short plot outlines (no more than a page), and a sample script or published story to show you understand comic book format. Again, there's no guarantee you'll receive an answer from an editor whose main concern is getting out his or her books.

Please send copies of your work (never send originals). DC Comics is not responsible for the safety or the return of any original material sent to us. It can take several weeks to evaluate your work. DO NOT PHONE to discuss your submission. We often receive hundreds of submissions a week, and it's impossible for us to deal with them over the phone.

If you have new properties or characters you'd like to propose, we suggest sending them to the editor whose published titles most closely represent the sensibility you feel your work demonstrates.

If you're planning to bring writing samples to a comics convention, keep in mind that it's difficult for an editor to give writing the attention it deserves in such a hectic, crowded environment. It's best to leave photocopies of your work with the editor for later review.

Breaking into comics as a writer is extraordinarily difficult. The big difference between submitting art and writing to DC Comics is this: We give new artists work based on the skills demonstrated in their samples, but we don't hire writers—we buy stories. It doesn't matter how skilled you are as a writer unless you can sell us a story idea.

Competition is fierce. DC publishes a limited number of titles and there are many people who want to write for them. Some established writers are not working up to capacity, and there are many would-be scripters waiting for their chance. Don't be discouraged. It's tough, but the best can find work at DC.

Story Formats

Full-length stories in DC's regular monthly titles range from 22 to 25, depending on format.

Be aware that no novice writer will be allowed to make major changes in continuity. Don't rely on new powers, death of an existing character, or personality changes to make your story compelling.

If your idea interests an editor, he or she will work with you on developing the idea further, either to plot or full script.

Professional work looks professional. Bad spelling, punctuation, and grammar are signs of the amateur. Editor will not be interested in proposals filled with errors.

All writing submissions must be TYPED double-spaced on one side of the paper. Hand-written submissions will not be considered.

Stylistic Requirements

Comic book writing is about telling a story in pictures, with words supplementing the visual storytelling. No matter what genre you want to work in, comic books convey, through pictures and words, action, movement, and urgency; a sense of drama and grandeur and "larger than life" excitement.

You should learn comic-book techniques and terminology and use them. *Comics and Sequential Art* by Will Eisner and *Understanding Comics* by Scott McCloud are excellent "bibles" for the conventions of the medium. If you have never seen how a comic book script is typically prepared, we suggest you purchase the trade paperback collection of *The Sandman: Dream Country,* which includes an annotated Neil Gaiman script.

Important Reminders

1. Always send photocopies; never send originals!

2. Include your name, address, and phone number on each page of your submission.

3. Always include a self-addressed stamped envelope with your submission, with sufficient U.S. postage or international reply coupon for a reply or the return of your copies (if you want them back).

4. Please handle all submissions-related correspondence with DC through the mail. Don't call.

GOOD LUCK!

DARK HORSE COMICS

(Please Note: This is a condensed version of the writer's guidelines, highlighting the more important areas. Send directly to Dark Horse Comics for a complete copy.)

It is the policy of Dark Horse Comics to secure a signed Submission Agreement before reviewing series, story and/or character proposals. If your desire is to only submit script samples, signing this agreement will not be necessary. If, however, your intention is to submit any original series, story, and/or character material, it will be necessary to submit a signed Submissions Agreement before any Dark Horse personnel will receive your proposal. Any submissions of original series, story, and/or character material that are not accompanied by a signed Submissions Agreement will be returned or destroyed without review. A Submissions Agreement can be acquired from the submissions editor with a SASE. Also, please note that Dark Horse will not review unsolicited story ideas or proposals pertaining to any licensed property currently published by Dark Horse (*Aliens, Predator, Terminator, Indiana Jones,* etc.) or any copyrighted or licensed property not owned by the submitter. Such material will be returned or destroyed without review.

- Signed Submission Agreement. Before Dark Horse will review an original proposal, a Submissions Agreement must be signed by the proposal's copyright holders and returned to Dark Horse.

- Cover Letter/Brief Overview. Very important. This is the sales pitch for your proposal. If it doesn't "grab" the editor, the remainder of the proposal will likely not be read. Make sure it is neatly typed—hand-written proposals will not be reviewed—and proofread for spelling and grammar; spelling and grammar errors give the impression that you're not a professional. Be clear, succinct, and cover all bases. Your cover letter must include:

  1. Current addresses and phone numbers of all collaborators, date of submission, working title of story or series you are submitting.

  2. Introduction with a brief list of published professional credits, if any, including those of any project collaborators.

  3. Brief story or series overview concentrating on central characters, themes, settings, and story situations and including the project's desired format (how many pages, issues, etc.) and the acceptable format alternatives.

- Complete Synopsis. Being as succinct as possible, this portion must include all important story elements. Tell the entire story—beginning, middle, and end. Avoid details that are absolutely not essential. A short-story synopsis should be not longer that one page. Synopsis for a series (limited or ongoing) or graphic novel should be no longer than five pages.

- Full Script. If you are a current published professional, you need not include a script of your proposed project, but you should include published examples of your best recent work with sample script for same. If you are not an established professional, you must include a full script for any short story or single-issue submission, or the first issue of any series. There are no exceptions to this rule. Proposals from unknown writers that do not include scripts will not be reviewed.

- Mailing and Packaging Requirements. Send proposals First Class Mail or Air Mail outside the U.S. Do not use Express Mail services. Include a self-addressed, stamped envelope with all submissions. DO NOT FAX PROPOSALS! Faxed unsolicited submissions will not be reviewed!

FANTAGRAPHICS BOOKS

When submitting work to Fantagraphics and Eros, for our convenience, please use standard size (8½" x 11") paper for all copies sent. Please address all submissions to "Submission Editor" and include a self-addressed stamped envelope (or an international reply coupon). Please do not send expensive packages. Likewise, it is unnecessary to send submissions by overnight mail, Federal Express, or courier. We judge your work according to its merits and our current needs, not according to attractive packaging that costs money.

We publish primarily black-and-white comics in standard comic format (6⅝" x 10¼"). We publish 24–32 page one-shots as well as series.

We prefer to see submissions from creators who can supply us with a complete project. We don't have the time or facilities to bring together writers, pencilers, inkers, etc. Please send a script or a rough synopsis of your idea, along with three to five finished pages from the story. This will give us a more accurate idea of your storytelling, drawing, and page layout skills than will unrelated drawings or sketches.

Please include a cover letter with your submission. We do not need to see a résumé.

It is quite difficult to generalize about the content of Fantagraphics comics. Briefly, I will say that we look for comics that are a product of a unique vision. We are not particularly interested in superheroes, sci-fi, fantasy, or other well-worn genres.

Eros submissions don't need to adhere to the thematic restrictions listed above. As a rule, there are no restrictions. We look for submissions of an "adult" nature that may range from soft-core erotica to hard-core pornography. A consensual and/or humorous approach is encouraged.

HARRIS COMICS

General Tips

Harris publishes the horror titles, *Creepy*, *Vampirella*, and *Eerie*, among others, so we are more interested in material with a horror or suspense angle than traditional superhero fare. However, we will look at superhero material if that's all you have in your portfolio at the moment. Make sure your submissions are neat and legible. Always send copies, never originals! A stamped, self-addressed envelope is a good way to ensure a prompt response. However, remember that we get a large volume of submissions and it is not unusual for us to take up to a month to respond. Particularly during convention season. DO NOT CALL THE OFFICE.

Writers
Enclose a brief summary or "springboard" of your story idea. Keep it short—a page or two is ideal. Leave the reader wanting to see more of your story, and stress an angle or hook that will distinguish your story or series idea from any other. Do not send full scripts.

KITCHEN SINK PRESS
The following are general rules to follow when submitting unsolicited freelance written proposals, synopses, and scripts to Kitchen Sink Press.

1. Enclose a self-addressed stamped envelope (SASE) with each submission. If you don't, your chances of a response are poor to nil. Enclosing a SASE saves us time, effort, and money. Nothing disturbs our editors more than disregarding this simple courtesy. We won't be responsible for either the care of the submission or a reply without a SASE.

2. Submissions must be typewritten and should be double-spaced.

3. We do not accept electronic submissions. We do not feel that this is an effective way to evaluate your work. Please do not send us submissions via e-mail or on disk. If you do, we will not review them.

4. We are open to reviewing any proposal having to do with comic material. We are not interested in books of text, per se, or in books of single-panel gag cartoons or in poetry. Our market is the comic book market, so proposals should fit that market.

5. We much prefer queries and/or synopses from first-time freelancers. Rather than wading through the pages of a speculative project, we would rather get the gist of an idea, a synopsis of a story. A one-page synopsis is usually sufficient. Accompanying art samples should be limited to approximately five pages (these are encouraged). If we like it, we will ask to see more. At that point, both parties are still not committed to buying or selling anything, but you certainly have our interest.

6. When submitting comic or graphic novel scripts, here are some procedures to follow:
   a. Scripts should be typewritten and double-spaced.
   b. Describe your characters as you introduce them. Give some background.
   c. Think visually. Words are important in comics, but many words can be eliminated with a visual panel.
   d. Each panel and/or scene should contain all the dialogue and/or narration for that panel.

7. Payment. Most titles are paid on a royalty basis, dependent on actual sales. Advances are paid against earned royalties. The exact terms will be negotiated when your submission is accepted for publication.

8. Copyrights. In the case of a writer collaborating with an artist, the copyright to a work is generally held by both. Copyrights to an individual's work are not held by Kitchen Sink Press.

MARVEL COMICS
(Please Note: Due to the length of Marvel's submissions guidelines, and the space constraints in this book, what follows is a condensed version of their guidelines highlighting the more important areas. Send directly to Marvel Comics for a complete copy.)

Who to Submit to
Address your submissions to "Submissions Editor." You may submit work to any other editor, but due to their heavy workloads, we cannot guarantee when (or even if) you'll get a response from any of them. The Submissions Editor will send you a response within four to six weeks, and will see to it that the rest of the editorial staff sees your work if it meets Marvel's current editorial needs.

New Characters

Do not submit new characters or proposals for new books to us. No one in the business makes a living just selling character ideas. Marvel characters are created and designed by the writers and artists of the books they appear in. Unless there is a contest, most editors won't even look at new character submissions for fear it might be similar to something already in development.

Important

Always enclose a self-addressed, stamped envelope large enough to return your submission and our response. Make certain your name and address are on every single page of your submission. Submissions without return postage will be regrettably discarded.

Before submitting material to a Marvel editor, call or write first to see if they are receptive to reading potential inventory material. The sheer volume of submissions Marvel gets these days has increased to the point that we can no longer devote any time to reading unsolicited material and will return all such material unread. Assuming an editor gives you the go-ahead, submit a synopsis of your plot idea no more than one-page (or one-paragraph) long. Editors have no time to read fully fleshed-out stories. If they like the synopsis, they give the go-ahead to submit the completed story and things proceed from there. Once you submit material, don't expect an immediate reply because editors usually give the lowest priority to submission answering (due to the fact that getting their books to the printer has to be the highest priority and takes most of their time.)

You can write a story about any Marvel character who has his or her own book, but if you want the story to be seriously considered for publication, you will write stories for titles that use inventory material on occasion. If a book has been written by the same person for several years, it is not likely that the editor of that title buys many inventory stories. Never submit stories featuring characters that do not have their own books. New books or limited series are never created just so we can buy a novice writer's story.

Submit short plot synopses only, double-spaced, no more than one page in length; establish the characters and the situation, introduce the conflict, and show the resolution. You may submit more than one plot synopsis at a time, but a dozen may tax an editor's patience. Do not submit detailed plots or full scripts until you have an editor's approval of your premise or rough synopsis.

Plot submissions should feature Marvel characters. We cannot buy any stories about characters Marvel doesn't own, nor can we judge how well you handle Marvel characters if you use characters that belong to someone else. Creating incidental characters or villains for your story is okay, but be aware that if we buy the story using them, Marvel will own those characters.

A regular monthly Marvel comic is 22 pages in length. Submit single-part stories that are self-contained. Never submit multi-part stories. Inventory stories requiring more than 22 pages or any other special format are never purchased from novice writers. Inventory plots for eight-page stories are viable as well. We hope this answers all your questions.

Good luck in future endeavors!

CONTRIBUTOR BIOGRAPHIES

Mike Baron started his professional comics writing career in 1982. His personal interests are broad and varied, and include motorcycling, reading, travel, and movies. He used to like building model cars, and claims that if he weren't writing comics he would probably be building model cars for a living, despite the fact that he seems to have no room for them in his house. Mike's credits include *Nexus* and *Badger* for Dark Horse, *The Punisher* for Marvel, *Bruce Lee* for Malibu, and *H.A.R.D. Corps* for Valiant. When Mike's not qualifying for the Nobel Peace Prize, he insists, "Talent is not enough, you have to work real hard at it." He lives not too far from Lake Wingra in southern Wisconsin.

Karen Berger started out as a comics professional in 1979. She says that despite the amount of time she's been an editor, it hasn't felt that long. She graduated from Brooklyn College as an English major with an Art History minor. Her editing credits for comics include the books featuring almost every character that ended up becoming a part of the DC Comics/Vertigo line, including *Swamp Thing* (with Alan Moore), *Hellblazer, Shade, Sandman, Animal Man, Books Of Magic, Black Orchid*, and the *Kid Eternity* mini-series. Karen started up each of the books (except *Swamp Thing*) with the respective writers. Currently she is the executive editor in charge of the Vertigo line for DC Comics, and she edits *Sandman* and *Sandman Mystery Theater.* Karen states enigmatically, "As someone famous once said, 'Truth is stranger than fiction.'" Karen has achieved a number of industry honors, including the Eisner Award for Best Editor (twice, and tied once with *Superman* editor, Mike Carlin). She has also won the *Comics Buyer's Guide* Favorite Editor Award. She also has received the YWCA's Women in Business Achievement Award. She loves to read and exercise, "when I get the chance."

Kurt Busiek's first professional work was a backup story for *Green Lantern,* in 1982. Since then he has gone on to be a prolific and popular comics writer. He was born in Boston, graduated from Syracuse University, and has worked as a literary agent and as a sales manager in addition to writing. Kurt's monumental list of credits includes *Green Lantern, World's Finest, Justice League of America, Legend of Wonder Woman* and *Valor* for DC Comics, *Liberty Project* for Eclipse, *Vampirella* for Harris, *Johnny Demon* for Dark Horse, *Spectacular Spider-Man, Web of Spider-Man, Darkman, Power Man/Iron Fist, Marvels* for Marvel Comics, *Teenagents* for Topps, plus *Youngblood Strikefile, Regulators,* and *Velocity* for Image. Kurt says, "If they'd told me there was going to be a quiz, I'd have studied harder!" He lives in the Pacific Northwest, home to great microbrews and lots of rain. His faithful canine sidekick is his Welsh corgi, Hector.

D.G. (don't guess) Chichester started out as a comics professional about 1985, following his earning of a Bachelor of Fine Arts in Film and Television from the NYU's Tisch School of the Arts. His leap into comics was preceded by a variety of part-time jobs, including the Hubba Bubba Gumfighter (when he handed out gum samples in shopping mall parking lots while dressed in elaborate cowboy regalia and a hugely oversized 10-gallon hat). His other interests include computer graphics, strange model kits, and, of course, his lovely wife Jennifer. "You know you've been spending too much time with technology when you find yourself reaching for the Undo command in real life," he muses. Dan's credits include *Marshal Law* and *Hellraiser* (editing) from Marvel/Epic; *Big Numbers* (production manager) from Mad Love Press; *Punisher/Captain America: Blood and Glory* (with Margaret Clark), *Feivel Goes West* comics adaptation, *Daredevil, Terror, Inc., Elektra: Root of Evil* and *Daredevil: Original Sin* (writer) all for Marvel Comics; *Classics Illustrated: Moby Dick* (with Bill Sienkiewicz) for First Comics; the *Motorhead* series from Dark Horse Comics; screenplays *Primal* and *Dark Lotus* (with Erik Saltzgaber). Dan lives in New York state with Jennifer and their black-and-white marshmallow cat, Slashing Claw, who completely lives down to his name. Now that he knows how to work his computer, Dan swears he'll never touch a T-square ever again.

Steve Englehart started writing for comics in 1970. His mentor was Neal Adams who, despite the fact that Steve was still in the army, encouraged him to come up to New York on weekends so that they could work together. As a result, once Steve left the army he already had some published work. His first solo work was done in the fall of 1971. He says wryly, "Me and Dan Quayle are the same age, from the same place, but they forgot to call me up and tell me about the National Guard!" He has a BA in Psychology, which he says stems from a desire to understand why people are the way they are. He says that this obviously led to his work as a writer since it provided him with an opportunity to explore just that. "I like to write characters. And I think the reason I do is because I like to get inside all the different personality types." His long comics career and vast number of projects includes *Strangers* and *Nightman* for Malibu Comics, *Captain America, Dr. Strange, Master of Kung Fu, Silver Surfer, Vision and the Scarlet Witch, Fantastic Four,* for Marvel Comics, *Millennium, Batman, Green Lantern Corps, Justice League of America,* for DC Comics and *Coyote* and *Scorpio Rose* for both Eclipse and Epic. He is also one of the seven "founding fathers" of Malibu's *Ultraverse* line, did the original stories and treatments that led to the first *Batman* movie, and designed a variety of videogames including the first *Spider-Man* game for Sega. He also writes a series of juvenile mysteries called *The DNAgers* through Avon. The television series based on his *Night Man* is now in its second season, and he is a continuing writer for it. *The Silver Surfer* animated series based on his comics run is currently on Fox. He is writing *Spider Noir*, a film noir *Spider-Man* novel for release in the year 2000. Steve lives in California with his wife, Terry, and their two sons, Alex and Eric. They also have a cat and a turtle. The turtle body surfs, but he never loses his keys.

Mark Evanier broke into comics in 1969. After a year or two at U.C.L.A., he spent a year "hanging around" Jack Kirby. He says he can't think of any way—past, present or future—to learn more about comics. Mark wrote for magazines and jokes for stand-up comics, before he started working in comics. He insists that he's fortunate in never having had to really work for a living. His comics cred-its include *Blackhawk* and *New Gods* (Writer) for DC Comics, *DNAgents* and *Crossfire* (writer, co-creator) for Eclipse, *Hollywood Superstars* for Epic/Marvel, *The Mighty Magnor* for Malibu Comics, *Groo the Wanderer* (with Sergio Aragones) for ImageComics, *Yogi Bear, Scooby-Doo, Bugs Bunny, Flintstones,* and *Daffy Duck* for Gold Key Comics, and *Mickey Mouse* and *Super Goof* for Disney. Some of his TV credits include *Welcome Back Kotter, Cheers, Bob, Love Boat, Garfield and Friends, Mother Goose and Grimm, ABC Weekend Special, Dungeons and Dragons,* and *Scooby-Doo.* Mark says, "Writing comics is like working on a Ouija board: When it works, it's like someone else guided your hands." Outside of comics, Mark has a plethora of interests including movies, TV, Broadway, politics, computers, journalism, Blackjack, and other games. He states that he has two bookcases full of Watergate books. He also has three Emmy nominations, one Inkpot award, and one Eisner award. Mark lives and works in Los Angeles, California, with his cat, Jack.

Neil Gaiman began his professional comics career in 1987. Considered by many to be one of the top writers in modern comics, he is also a best-selling novelist. He is responsible for an impressive list of record-breaking comic sales and industry awards (much too extensive to list here), and his work has been translated into more than eight languages. Neil's comics credits include *Black Orchid, Violent Cases, Death: The High Cost of Living, Sandman* series and collections, *Mr. Punch* and *The Last Temptation* for DC Vertigo, *Signal to Noise* (illustrated by Dave McKean) for *Gollancz,* and *Miracleman: The Golden Age* for Eclipse and HarperCollins. Noteworthy prose work includes *Angels and Visitations* from DreamHaven, and novels *Good Omens* (with Terry Pratchett), *Ghastly beyond Belief, Don't Panic,* and *Neverwhere.* Neil was born in 1960 and tends to need a haircut. He currently calls America home.

Dave Gibbons started his professional comics career as an artist in 1973 and as a writer in 1989. He says he was educated at a traditional English school, all dreaming spires and black gowns. Art was frowned upon. In the early 1970s, he qualified as a surveyor, but only worked in that field (and he means field) for a couple of years. "This, too, will pass," he says ruminatively. Dave states that as far as comic art goes, he's self-taught, and he believes that the qualities of storytelling in his art have lulled editors into thinking he can also write. He claims to have never made an unsolicited submission in his professional comics career. Dave's credits include the art on *The Watchmen* and writing on *World's Finest* and *Superman: Kal* for DC Comics, writing on *Rogue Trooper* for Fleetway Comics and *Tundra*, art work for *Give Me Liberty* and *Martha Washington Goes to War* and writing on *Aliens: Salvation* for Dark Horse Comics. Dave is interested in computer graphics and loves to travel (though mainly to conventions, it seems). He has also trained in tai chi for about five years. Dave lives with his wife, Kate, and son, Daniel, in Hertfordshire, England.

Lurene Haines has been a comics professional since 1986. She moved to the U.S.A. from her home of Victoria, British Columbia, after completing a Bachelor of Science degree, to work as the art assistant and business manager for a comic artist. In 1988 she left Seattle, Washington, to work as a freelance writer and artist. Lurene's work spans comics, magazines, newspapers, books, trading cards, and toy designs. Some of her credits include *Green Arrow: The Longbow Hunters* for DC Comics, *Hellraiser* for Epic Comics, *Indiana Jones* and *The Fate of Atlantis* for Dark Horse Comics, *Ms. Fury* and *Star Trek: Deep Space Nine* for Malibu Entertainment, *Star Wars Galaxy* trading cards for Topps, *Thumbscrew, Femina,* and *Femina Two* for Caliber Comics, and she wrote and edited *Star Wars: The Art of Dave Dorman* for FPG/Random House. Her first book, *The Business of Comics* is an in-depth manual for aspiring comics professionals, and has garnered extensive critical acclaim and an Eisner award nomination. Haines is currently working as a children's book writer and illustrator, and has a business designing and building Internet web pages. Visit Lurene's web site at http://www.hainesworld.com to see a gallery of her art and writing. Lurene shares a home and studio with her kooky cats, Frankie and Nemo.

Tony Isabella started out as a comics professional, working for Marvel, in the fall of 1972, following a three-year stint with *The Cleveland Plain Dealer.* Since then he has also worked as an editor at DC Comics, as a comic retailer, a distributor, a show promoter, and an industry consultant. Tony is a prolific writer, who has worked with most of the major comic publishers. Tony states, "Editors and publishers are rarely as professional as they expect you to be." His credits include *Avengers, Spider-Man, Daredevil, Ghost Rider,* and *Dracula* for Marvel, *Hawkman* and *Black Lightning* for DC Comics, *Satan's Six* for Topps, and *Justice Machine* for Comico. He has also been a regular column contributor for the *Comics Buyer's Guide* for over 10 years. Tony spends a lot of time researching his writing work and can sometimes even be found in Cleveland's inner city doing research for his *Black Lightning* stories. He says that between raising his kids, Eddie and Kelly Rose, and doing his writing and research, he doesn't have much time for special interests. However when pressed, he confesses to a special interest in goofy old comics from the 1960s. Tony lives in Ohio with his sainted wife Barb and their two children.

Dan Jurgens began working in comics in 1982. He received his BFA in Graphic Design from the Minneapolis College of Art. As a student intern he began working as a "living, breathing, functioning graphic designer" for a defense contractor, where he stayed on after college, for about three years. When asked about his "big break" in comics, Dan says "Mike Grell [artist/writer] was traveling through town making personal appearances, and I stopped in and showed him my work. A couple of months later I was drawing *Warlord* for him. It was fairly easy for me to get into comics compared to what a lot of people go through." Dan followed up his work on *Warlord* with a variety of projects for DC Comics including *Superman* (writing and drawing), the *Zero Hour* mini-series (writing and drawing), *Justice League* (writing and drawing), *Green Arrow* (drawing), the *Flash Gordon* mini-series (writing and drawing), and creating the *Booster Gold* series which he also wrote and drew. His upcoming projects include a *Superman/Aliens* crossover, which he is also writing and drawing, with inks provided by Kevin Nowlan for DC Comics and Dark Horse Comics. Dan says, "We as an industry tend to take ourselves way to seriously at times. When I see new work—whether it's writing or art samples—it tends to be from guys who come up with great big, grandiose changes for a character. I would prefer to see approaches from new people that bring the fun back into it [comics]." Dan makes his home in the Twin Cities area of Minnesota with his wife, Ann Merrill, their two sons, Quinn and Seth, and the family cat, Corky.

Denis Kitchen began his lengthy tenure as a comic professional in 1969. His colorful and respected history in the industry has been summarized in *Kitchen Sink Press: The First 25 Years* (Kitchen Sink Press). His self-publishing skills began in grade school, and commercial illustration provided him income from the age of 13. In college, knowing he wanted to be a cartoonist, he chose to major in journalism to learn communication skills as there were no specialized classes for aspiring comic book writers or artists in the 1960s. His artistic skills are self-taught. With the formation of Kitchen Sink Press in 1969, Denis found his first and last job. He has the distinction of being the only cartoonist who has also owned and operated retail, distribution, and publishing businesses. "Writers must remember that they have to grab the comic reader by the eyeballs," he insists. Denis collects vintage juke boxes, 1940s and 1950s tin cars, robots, and cartoon character toys. Some of the prestigious features produced by his company include Will Eisner's graphic novel series *A Contract with God, A Life Force*, and *To the Heart of the Storm, Xenozoic Tales* (a.k.a. *Cadillacs & Dinosaurs)* by Mark Schultz, *From Hell* by Alan Moore and Eddie Campbell, *Blood Club* and *Black Hole* by Charles Burns, *Understanding Comics* by Scott McCloud, and *The Crow* by James O'Barr. They have also published collections of classic comics and strips by Harvey Kurtzman, Alex Raymond, Milton Caniff, Al Capp, and others. Denis lives and works in a beautiful area of Massachusetts, where he is endlessly pruning and carving paths in his private woods as an escape from the business world.

Joe R. Lansdale started his professional comics writing career around 1991. Before taking a shot at comics, he had been writing prose professionally since 1973. "I'm just a small-town Texas boy who grew up readin' comics," Joe states matter-of-factly. "Comics had as much influence on me as anything else, although I primarily think of myself as a prose writer. Comics are what excited me, and fired my imagination." After all that comics reading, Joe went on to do a variety of odd jobs to make a living including working in an aluminum chair factory, as a janitor, and writing book reviews for a small weekly paper before beginning his professional writing career. His comic and prose credits include *Jonah Hex: Two Gun Mojo, Jonah Hex: Riders of the Worm* and *Blood and Shadows* (artist, Mark Nelson) for DC Comics, *The Lone Ranger: It Crawls* for Topps Comics, *Tarzan's Lost Adventure* for Dark Horse Comics, *Mucho Mojo* (novel), *Two Bear Mambo* (novel), *Savage Season* (novel), and *Cold in July* (novel) from Mysterious Press, *Writer of the Purpler Rage* (short story collection) for CD Publications, and *Batman: Captured by the Engines* for Warner Books. Joe lives with his lovely wife, Karen, children Keith and Kasey, and his German Shepherd, Cooter, deep in the heart of Texas.

David Lloyd officially started work as a comics professional in 1977. Although he's been drawing comics since he was 13, he didn't go to art school. He says he regrets that, not for the loss of art education but because he missed out on the social fun. His training began as a commercial artist in a studio that specialized in advertising art, where he started out as a messenger and tea boy. After about two and a half years, he moved up to working on the drawing board. David drew comic strips in his spare time and on lunch hours for fun, but says his co-workers didn't take the comics seriously although they did seem to enjoy them. After six years he left to try his hand at freelance illustration on book covers and children's books. However, he claims quite bluntly that he couldn't get work because he was "basically no good." Once reaching that realization, he spent the next four years dividing his time between teaching himself to be a better artist through practice and study, and part-time jobs working in a cabinetmakers workshop and as a painter and decorator in a department store. Throughout that time he continued to draw comic strips, and finally got work with a British publisher of children's comics. Once he got his first job, David says he started working on comics full-time.

David says with passion, "I love drawing comics. I love telling stories. To me it's the closest thing to doing a movie, and that's what I like about it most of all." His comic credits include *V for Vendetta* and *The Horrorist* from DC Comics, *Night Raven: House of Cards* from Marvel Comics, *Philip Marlowe: The Pencil* for Byron Preiss, and *James Bond: Shattered Helix* and *Hard Looks* for Dark Horse Comics. David spends a portion of his time teaching classes at the London Cartoon Center and makes his home in jolly old England.

Bill Messner-Loebs slid into comics professionalism in 1982. That was the first year that his creation, *Journey,* was published. But before beginning a career in comics, Bill felt he pretty much couldn't get arrested. He tried homesteading along the Canadian border with some friends, was involved in a very sort-lived and unsuccessful catamaran-building business, and worked in an art supply store and custom framing shop for a couple of years. In his words, "it was all sort of grungy retail stuff." Then, for about 10 years he tried sending out samples while enjoying his parent's hospitality. Obviously, he was ultimately successful. Bill's credits include *Journey* from Fantagraphics, *Johnny Quest* from Comico, as well as *Wonder Woman* and *Hawkman* from DC Comics. Bill's next project, *Bliss Alley: Alchemy at Street Level* is currently in development. Bill says, cheerfully, "We all fall off the planet sooner than we expect. Have fun!" He currently lives with his wife, Nadine, in the natural wilds of Michigan.

Roland Mann began his professional career in comics as a writer in 1988. After a successful run self-publishing his popular creation *Cat and Mouse,* (which was later published by Malibu's Aircel line), Roland was offered a job as an editor for the California-based Malibu Comics in 1990. He took the job somewhat hesitantly, being a true-blue Mississippi boy, born and bred. It was at the University of Southern Mississippi that Roland got his BS in English. But, he relocated to Southern California despite fears about earthquakes, which were horribly realized in 1994 with the devastating quake that was centered at his new home. He claims that it was a good thing the airlines weren't flying, or he and his wife would have jumped a plane and headed back home to Mississippi. Since then, life has settled down to occasional, tolerable aftershocks. Roland's code for happiness and success is, "Surround yourself with cool people who share your interests," and he thoughtfully maintains, "Read, read, read. Never forget to educate yourself." Roland's credits include *Miss Fury,* the *Genesis* line *(Protectors, Ferret, Ex-mutants,* etc.), the *Ultraverse* line (including *Sludge* and *Nightman),* and *Battletech* for Malibu Comics. After corporate layoffs, Roland found himself back home in Mississippi with his smart, beautiful wife, B.J. and daughter Brittany. His latest writing projects are *Switchblade, Silverstorm, Beah,* and others, as well as running the small press comic publishing company Silverline.

Tom Mason had his first script published in 1987. His job was to dialogue a comic called *Battle to the Death #3.* "It's still one of the funniest things I ever worked on," says Tom. "It was also the first time that Chris Ulm [former Malibu Editor-in-Chief] and I ever worked together on a project." Before comics, he supported himself in college by working in a grocery store. He also worked in a museum, drove a restaurant delivery van, and collected unemployment. Tom claims to have no background experience that prepared him for writing, except that he always knew he wanted to be a writer and wrote every chance he got. He was on the staff of his high school yearbook, and wrote regularly for his college newspaper. He was a gag writer for a disc jockey, a cartoonist for *Playboy* and *Cosmopolitan* magazines (among many), and a freelance reviewer. Tom was the Creative Director for Malibu Comics, and now is maniacally busy with his new company, MainBrain productions, which he co-founded with Chris Ulm and Dan Danko. His comic credits include creating Malibu's *Dinosaurs for Hire* and co-creating *Prototype* for Malibu's *Ultraverse,* in addition to editing a vast array of Malibu titles. "Never take your hamster to the vet," Tom grins. "For five bucks you can get a new one." Tom's other interests include reading just about anything he can get his hands on. He writes everyday, even when he doesn't have a deadline or assignment. He also likes to sleep, but says, "opportunities rarely present themselves these days." Tom lives and works in sunny Southern California with a fish that swims upside down and does a very good impersonation of floating death.

John Moore started his professional work in comics in 1985 as an art assistant to Howard Chaykin. He began writing professionally in 1987. After getting a degree in Illustration and Graphic Design from Cal State University, Fullerton, he worked as a technical illustrator for an environmental consulting firm for six months. Then he returned to working with Howard Chaykin. John says that comics have been a regular thing since then, paying the bills, even when he was "hustling screen work." "I did manage to avoid having to do food service," he states happily, "post-college I was doing pretty much art or writing." He laughs, "I'm pretty unprepared to do anything else except go back to school and get a graduate degree! But I've worked hard, and I've had a lot of opportunities come my way without having to scramble or climb for them. I've been pretty fortunate." He says he hasn't done art in a while but is actually "planning to do something." John's comic credits include *American Flagg! Vol #2* for First Comics, *Superboy, Ironwolf: Fires of the Revolution* (with Howard Chaykin), *Batman/Houdini: The Devil's Workshop* (with Chaykin), and *Under a Yellow Sun: A Novel By Clark Kent*, and *Chronos* for DC Comics, *Doom 2099, X-Men 2099, X-Men Unlimited, X-Force* and *X-Factor* for Marvel Comics. His work for television includes executive story consultant for *The Flash* (with Chaykin) and writing episodes of *Human Target, The Palace Guard* (both with Chaykin), and *Viper*. "Dignity, always dignity," John says, quoting Gene Kelly from *Singing in the Rain*. John lives in San Francisco, where he's required by city law to wear black and frequent coffee houses.

Clydene Nee started her professional career in comics around 1989, but has been involved in comics through convention work since 1978. Clydene says that much of her knowledge about art and painting comes from her mother, Mrs. Rayme Nee, who immersed her in art. She taught both occupational art and art classes for school children. As early as age three, Clydene remembers her mother dragging her and her siblings to art museums and spending a lot of time looking at art books. The smell of turpentine and oils was very common around her house. Her mother taught her about the four-color process early on with scraps of color-proofing material from a local printer, and showed her how to combine colors with clay and playdough. For a number of years, Clydene has been the Art Auction/Artist's Alley Coordinator for the San Diego Comic Convention. She enjoys the fact that now, as a professional, she has the opportunity to work with pros who were her "heroes" as she grew up. She has two degrees from U.C.S.D. in Political Science and History, with a minor in Economics, and started an MBA in Management Information Systems. She has two certificates from IBM for computer training and has worked as a technical writer/illustrator for a computer software company. Clydene's professional credits include work as colorist and color separator on *Ultraman* and *SeaQuest* for Harvey Comics, *Images of Shadowhawk* for Image's Shadowline, *Image Universe* Cards for Topps, and *Hellshock #2* and *Image #0* for Image. She has worked for Dark Horse Comics, Image, Comico, Now Comics, Hero, Malibu Comics, Harvey Comics, Wildstorm Productions, and Top Cow. Clydene lives and works very, very hard in Southern California.

John Ostrander began his professional comics career about 1982. Prior to that, John went into professional theater directly from college, working miscellaneous other jobs to support his "theater habit." He worked as an actor, director, playwright, producer ("very badly"), and as an acting coach. He also hung lights and built sets. "There was nothing in professional theater that I didn't do," he claims. He worked primarily for First Comics at the beginning of his career, then shifted over to DC Comics as he got to know people there. Since then he has gone on to be a popular and prolific comics writer. Some of his industry credits include *Suicide Squad* (with Kim Yale), *Wasteland, Firestorm, The Spectre*, and *Gotham Nights II* for DC Comics, *Magnus Robot Fighter, Rai*, and *Eternal Warrior* for Valiant, *Elf Quest: Jink* for Warp Graphics, *Grimjack* for First Comics, a *Bishop* mini-series, and a *Wolverine* graphic novel (with Tom Mandrake) for Marvel Comics. John also teaches comics writing classes at the New York School of Visual Arts (with Denny O'Neill) and at The Joe Kubert School for Cartooning. One of John's other passions is beer-making, at which he's "pretty darn good. It's part science, part art, and part pure magic. And a whole lot of fun!" He claims to make "strange and interesting brews" and brags about his cherry and jalapeno beers. "Writing comics is terrific," John says conspiratorially, "They give me lots of money to do something I have a lot of fun doing." He lives in New Jersey with his talented and lovely wife, author Kim Yale.

Scott Peterson got his start in comics in 1991. A restless soul, Scott was born in Dallas, grew up in northern Connecticut, and went to college in Virginia for a long, long time. He then began working for DC Comics where he is now an editor and Batman Group Liaison. Some of his editorial credits include *Detective Comics, Batman Adventures, Green Arrow, The Huntress,* and *Batman v. Predator II* all for DC Comics. He was extremely fortunate to have Brian Stelfreeze draw an *Oracle* story, which he wrote, and was recently published. Brian and Scott are talking about working together again. In the meantime, he continues to get ulcers. He says with some humor and reverence, "I continue to be astonished at what a genius Alan Moore is." Scott lives in New York City with his wife and over 100 houseplants—98 more than he'd like.

Jerry Prosser started out as a comics professional in 1989. He came up through the editorial ranks at Dark Horse Comics, starting work with them when the company was about one-year old. From that experience of being in the business and learning the ropes, he started seriously working on scripting for comics. He believes that being in the professional environment of a publisher put him in the fortuitous position of learning the trade and skills of writing for comics. Jerry currently works full-time as a freelance writer, and his credits include *Exquisite Corpse, Aliens: Hive, Cyberantics,* and *Predator: Invaders from the Fourth Dimension* from Dark Horse Comics, *Animal Man* and *Skin Graft: Adventures of a Tattooed Man* from DC's Vertigo line, and Bram Stoker's *Burial of the Rats* from Cosmic. Jerry also has a Masters degree in Social Work, about which he laughingly says, "I think it prepared me to work with disturbed individuals, which is perfect for the comics market." He is a

self-described bibliophile and popular culture junkie admitting to being influenced by everything from the Fortean phenomenon, Italian spaghetti westerns, J.G. Ballard, Rudy Ray Moore, and William S. Burroughs to the Michelin Man and Reddy Kilowatt. He currently lives in Oregon with his beautiful and talented wife Ronnie Noize, and two slightly neurotic dogs.

Joe Pruett started working as a comics professional in 1989, while working with Bob Burden on *Flaming Carrot Comics*. His first published work as a writer was in *Calibrations #1* in 1992 with the first appearance of his creation, *Kilroy*. His first published work as an editor was *Negative Burn* in 1993. Joe has an English degree from the University of Georgia. His editorial credits include *Moebius Comics, The Bandy Man, Kingdom of the Wicked* from Caliber Comics. His writing credits include *Kilroy Is Here, Untouchables,* and *Exit* (creator/ writer) from Caliber Press, *Dusty Star* and *The Nameless* for Image Comics, and *Avalon* for Sirius Entertainment. Currently, Joe is the Creative Director for Caliber Comics. Joe says, "If you believe in yourself and demonstrate an outward confidence then others will come to be confident in you as well. You can do anything you want if you believe in yourself. I'm living my dream everyday." Joe lives just outside Ann Arbor, Michigan, with his wife, Melissa and daughter Hannah, and is always eager to point out that he is the "better looking" twin compared to his brother, James.

Kelley Puckett started his comics career in 1990 as an assistant editor to Denny O'Neil. He got his staff position at DC Comics about a week after graduation, before which he had done a little computer programming as a summer job. In 1991 he branched into freelance work, which he now enjoys full-time. Kelley enjoys movies, particularly Hitchcock, martial arts—which he used to instruct before becoming swamped with work, cosmology, and particle physics (layman's level). His comic credits include *Green Arrow, Batman Adventures, Superman & Batman* all for DC Comics. Kelley says some of the best advice he ever got was from Larry Niven: "Never lose your sense of imagination." Kelley currently lives his very private life in San Francisco.

Mark "The Madman" Ricketts took on the comics industry as a professional in November 1992, purportedly the "winter of his discontent." He wildly claims that his family is made up of hand-waving tellers of elaborate stories, mile-a-minute jabber jaws, and bold-faced liars, and that he was born to be either a used car salesman or a writer. He chose the latter. Mark's extensive list of independent credits includes *Warpwalking, International Cowgirl Magazine, Twilight People,* a *Twilight People* serial in *Negative Burn #9-13, The Book of Twilight* trade paperback, *Nowheresville,* work in *Deadworld, Thumbscrew, The Lost,* and *High Caliber* all for Caliber Press, as well as a short story in *Urban Legends,* a pin-up in Mike Mignola's *Hellboy* both for Dark Horse Comics, and illustrations for a collection of *Ambrose Bierce* stories for Mojo Press. He states most firmly, yet with his ever-present mischievous leer, "Every writer I know is an insecure, inhibited voyeur. You'd swear they were aliens gathering information about our planet to bring back to their home world." Although his place of origin remains a mystery to those who know him, he currently hides out in Illinois.

Mark Schultz began his professional comics career in 1986. Prior to working in comics, Mark graduated from Kutztown State College with a BFA in painting. He tried working as a fine art painter for a while, but laughingly says, "It wore real thin, real quick." He did commercial art for a number of years, including book illustration and advertising art. He found it dissatisfying, however, because of a yearning to tell stories. At that point he took the plunge into comics. His professional credits include creating, writing and artwork for *Xenozoic Tales* published by Kitchen Sink Press. It has gone on to be adapted as *Cadillacs & Dinosaurs,* which is a color comic from Topps, an animated TV series produced by Nelvana, a CD-ROM game, and a line of action-figure toys from Tyco. In addition to his *Xenozoic Tales* commitments, Mark has written a *Flash Gordon* story (illustrated by Al Williamson) for Marvel Comics. Mark says, "At *Xenozoic Tales* our guarantee to you, the reader, is that we'll always deliver more value for your entertainment dollar!" He lives with his very captivating wife, Denise, and a plethora of fantasy dinosaurs, in the heart of Pennsylvania.

Diana Schutz became a comics professional in 1984. After receiving a Bachelor in Fine Arts with a major in creative writing from the University of British Columbia, she dropped out of grad school in 1978 to sell comics at The Comicshop in Vancouver, B.C. In 1981 she moved to California and began working at the Berkeley store of the Comics & Comix chain. Within six months, she started up *The Telegraph Wire,* a newsletter for the chain, and also freelanced interviews, articles, and reviews for the *Comics Buyer's Guide, The Comics Journal,* and *Amazing Heroes.* From there, she moved to New York in 1984 and was offered a job at Marvel Comics, where she worked for one brief week before she quit. "I was a little girl, and I couldn't believe that pie-in-the-sky Marvel Comics had offered me a job. Imagine my surprise to get there and find it was a real midtown-Manhattan corporation! It was just not for this ol' hippie." She then accepted a job with Comico based in Norristown, Pennsylvania. Diana worked with Comico from 1985 to 1989, followed by a year of freelancing, during which Comico continued to be one of her clients. In March of 1990, Diana came to work with the rapidly growing Dark Horse Comics. She worked as Managing Editor for about a year, but stepped down because she realized she missed hands-on editing. She worked as an editor for the next three years before Dark Horse enticed her back into management. During her time at Dark Horse Comics, Diana also went back to school part-time, and taking one course per semester over three and a half years, managed to complete a Master of Arts in Communication Studies at the University of Portland. Her thesis was on female cartoonists. Diana's professional credits include editing *Grendel, Mage, Jonny Quest, Rio, Batman/Grendel,* and *Night and the Enemy* (with Harlan Ellison) for Comico, as well as *Grendel, Rio, American Splendor, Batman/Predator, Barry Windsor-Smith: Storyteller,* and, most recently, *Sin City* for Dark Horse. She also proofreads on a freelance basis for such clients as Dave Sim and Steve Bisette. Diana says she has a lot of "significant persons" in her life, but for now she only shares her Portland, Oregon, home with her cats, Mouse and Easy.

Louise Simonson started her professional comics writing career in 1984. She started out as an editor in 1974 at Warren Publishing, working on *Creepy, Eerie,* and *Vampirella.* She became a senior editor in 1976, and then was hired by Marvel Comics in 1980. There, she edited *X-Men, New Mutants, Conan, Star Wars, Battlestar Galactica, Star Trek, Indiana Jones* and *Man Thing.* Once she began writing she produced stories for *X-Factor, Power Pack, Meltdown, Web of Spiderman, New Mutants,* and *Red Sonja* for Marvel, plus *Batman, Superman: Man of Steel* and *Steel* for DC Comics. She has also written a *Star Wars* mini-series for Dark Horse Comics. In addition to her comics work, Louise has been producing a variety of children's books, including *Superman: Doomsday and Beyond* for Warner Books, *I Hate Superman* for Little Brown, plus *Superman* and *Wonder Woman* for Little Golden Books. "A good editor is worth his/her weight in gold," says Louise, "and Mike Carlin [*Superman* editor for DC Comics] is worth twice his weight in gold!" When not engrossed in her writing work, her husband Walter states that she reads an astounding amount, and Louise says she enjoys histories, historical romances, biographies, mysteries, and some science fiction. "Children's books, I just love children's books," she says. Louise lives with her talented husband, Walter Simonson, in New York State.

Len Strazewski started working as a comics professional around 1984, although he has been making money as a professional writer since the tender age of 19. He is primarily a journalist, but worked as a business journalist and magazine editor until he started making "big" money in comics. To date, journalism still accounts for about half of his working time, and his writing includes features on computer technology and employee benefits. Len has a Bachelors in journalism from Northwestern University, a Masters in creative writing from the University of Illinois, and a Masters in Industrial Relations from Loyola University. Len's comics credits include *Justice Society of America, Starman* and *The Flash* for DC Comics, in addition to *The Fly* and *The Web* for their Impact Line, *Speed Racer* and *Die Kamikaze* for Now Comics, as well as editing and creative consulting for *Trollords* from Tru Studios, then Comico, and finally Apple Comics. Len is also one of the seven "founding fathers" of Malibu's *Ultraverse* line and is co-creator of *Prime* (with Gerard Jones) and *Prototype* (with Tom Mason). He also has written a new *Ultraverse* mini-series, *Elven.* Len is developing *Hero Cycle,* a "creative landscape" he hopes will be used in all aspects of marketing—from action figures aimed at children to corporate assertiveness-training videos. Len says wryly, "Comics break my heart." To ease the pain, he has been enjoying acting as a mentor to some new young writers that he has recommended to Malibu and is working on a number of co-written stories with these new talents for *Ultraverse Premiere.* Len says he's had the same girlfriend for 11 years, with whom he celebrates mysterious anniversaries. He currently lives in Chicago, but is out in LA "an awful lot."

Rob Wood was kind enough to provide the short article about computer on-line copyright law. He is a freelance writer, editor, author, and publisher working in San Francisco. Rob says, "I don't really have a connection to comics (other than having read thousands of comic books in my youth)." He can be reached on the Internet at rwood@hypergold.com or visit his web site at http://www.hypergold.com.

INDEX

Page numbers in *italics* indicate artwork.

ILLUSTRATION CREDITS

Angelus © 1995 Lurene Haines.

Batman Promotional Poster © 1994 DC Comics. All Rights Reserved.

Batman Adventures #29 © 1994 DC Comics. All Rights Reserved.

Black Lightning #1 © 1994 DC Comics. All Rights Reserved.

Blood and Shadows © 1995 Mark Nelson and Joe Lansdale.

Caricature of Diana Schutz by Matt Wagner © 1995 Matt Wagner.

Caricature of Tom Mason by Patrick Owsley © 1995 Tom Mason.

Cyberantics artwork © 1995 Rick Geary.

Groo The Wanderer © 1995 Sergio Aragones.

Ironwolf: Fires of the Revolution © 1992 DC Comics. All Rights Reserved.

Journey © 1985 William Messner-Loebs.

Kilroy Is Here artwork © 1995 Andrew Robinson.

Martha Washington Saves the World™ © 1994 Frank Miller and Dave Gibbons.

Nexus:™ *Into the Vortex* © 1995 Mike Baron and Steve Rude.

RUNE and the distinctive likenesses thereof are trademarks of Marvel Comics Entertainment, Inc. © 1995.

Sandman: The Kindly Ones #66 © 1993 DC Comics. All Rights Reserved.

Sandman Mystery Theater Poster © 1993 DC Comics. All Rights Reserved.

Superman: The Man of Steel Annual #4 © 1994 DC Comics. All Rights Reserved.

Superman #82 © 1994 DC Comics. All Rights Reserved.

Switchblade © 1998 Silverline Comics.

Terror Tots™ © 1996 Len Strazewski and Paul Fricke.

The Specter #0 © 1994 DC Comics. All Rights Reserved.

The Book of Twilight © 1994 Mark Ricketts.

Ultrascarce Cover Parody © 1997 Steve Englehart.

Xenozoic Tales artwork © 1995 Mark Schultz.